SAINTE-MÈRE-ÉGLISE
THE 82ND U.S. AIRBORNE DIVISION

An 82nd U.S. Airborne patrol on its way up the main street in Sainte-Mère.
Four paras on spoiled horses. © NARA

Christophe PRIME and Éric BELLOC

SAINTE-MÈRE-ÉGLISE
THE 82ND U.S. AIRBORNE DIVISION

OREP
EDITIONS

CONTENTS

INTRODUCTION .... P. 6

CHAPTER 1: THE U.S. AIRBORNE ARMY .... P. 9

CHAPTER 2: EARLY COMBAT .... P. 25

CHAPTER 3: BY THE LONGEST NIGHT .... P. 41

CHAPTER 4: THE BATTLE OF SAINTE-MÈRE-ÉGLISE .... P. 65

CHAPTER 5: AFTER THE BATTLE .... P. 113

MAP OF OPERATIONS .... P. 126

BIBLIOGRAPHY .... P. 127

ACKNOWLEDGEMENTS .... P. 127

A medical unit from the 325th GIR patiently waiting on the airfield tarmac for the time to come to board. © NARA

6 June 1944. Glider troops from the 325th gearing up next to their gliders. In the background, the man with a bazooka on his shoulder is probably posing for a war photographer. © NARA

INTRODUCTION

On the 6th of June 1944, the American people learned that the long-awaited landings on the French coast had begun. Just like the codenamed beaches, they also heard of a small village called Sainte-Mère-Église. Troopers and gliders from the 82nd U.S. Airborne Division - who had already fought in Sicily and Salerno - were to face an ordeal of bitter combat to keep control of this strategic target.

Whilst the battle of Sainte-Mère-Église is considered to be one of the unit's major feats of arms, our aim is also to retrace the early days of the U.S. American airborne army and the many operations in which the All Americans participated during the Second World War.

The parachutist had no fallback solution. His mission was to fight to the enemy's rear and to accomplish the tasks he had been set, whatever the cost.

Christophe Prime

Did you know, for example, that the troopers and gliders from the 82nd Airborne Division continued to fight in Normandy as infantrymen up to mid-July, and that they were also engaged in the Battle of the Bulge, entrusted with blocking three German armoured divisions whilst the 101st U.S. Airborne held Bastogne?

Sainte-Mère-Église's renown has continuously grown over the years, to offer the village pride of place among the leading memorial sites of the Battle of Normandy. To this very day, there is an intimately fraternal link between this small French village and America, and with its sons, the famous All Americans.

Non-commissioned airborne army officers training on the use of the bayonet at Fort Benning. © NARA

CHAPTER 1

THE U.S. AIRBORNE ARMY

ORIGINS

On the 1st of March 1912, Captain Albert Berry made the very first parachute jump from a plane in flight during a demonstration above St. Louis (Missouri). Wearing a parachute attached to a static line, Berry jumped into the void, under the spectators' bewildered gaze. © NARA

The U.S. Army was the first to form an Air Infantry as from 1918.

Brigadier General William 'Bille' Mitchell suggested that the 1st U.S. Infantry Division be withdrawn from the Meuse-Argonne front and offered training in parachute jumping, so that they could be dropped behind the German lines to facilitate the capture of the fortress of Metz. The operation was scheduled for the spring of 1919. It was to mobilise 1,200 Handley Page O/400 bombers. Once on the ground, the troops would need to be supplied by the air and covered by fighter planes.

However, hostilities came to an end before the operation could be launched.

Due to drastic cuts in the armed forces' budget at the end of the war, Mitchell's visionary idea fell into oblivion. It was only in April 1928 that the first tactical test, involving men equipped with manually-operated parachutes, was conducted at Kelly Field. In 1932, an infantry unit was dropped during manoeuvres. The following year, an entire artillery battalion was transported by air during an exercise in Panama.

These decisive exercises convinced the U.S. Army and U.S. Air Corps leaders of the pertinence of creating parachute units, each one eager to command them, hence delaying the implementation of this new military tool. The U.S. Marine Corps also paid an interest. Meanwhile, foreign armies conducted their own experiments. In the 1930s, the Italians experimented with military parachutists, developing adequate material and techniques; however, the Soviets were the first to deploy the concept on a large scale. A parachute battalion was formed as early as 1929. The Irvin parachute was adopted in 1933 and the 3rd Airborne Brigade was created. Concurrently, they

At the end of the First World War, Brigadier General William Mitchell was in command of the U.S. Air Force in Europe. © NARA

developed airlanding and airdropping. Over the summer of 1935, the Soviet high command invited military observers to travel to Kiev to attend major manoeuvres involving over 6,000 parachutists. These large-scale exercises sent a shock wave running through the foreign delegations. As from the month of September, the *Luftwaffe* created a parachute regiment (*Fallschirmjäger*) on a voluntary basis. In France, the first military parachute centre was founded. The first two French air infantry groups (GIA) were created two years later.

The United States followed close in the footsteps of the European powers. General George Marshall, at the time U.S. Army Chief of Staff, requested that Major General George Lynch consider the creation of a parachute corps. He knew he could count on support from Major William C. Lee, who had attentively observed the development of the first parachute units in Germany.

Major airborne manoeuvres organised in the Kiev sector in 1935 generated a shock wave among the continental European and American armies. © Ivan Shagin/Sputnik

WILLIAM CAREY LEE (1895-1948)

William C. Lee was born in North Carolina and served as Second Lieutenant in the U.S. Infantry. He was sent to the European front in 1917. At the end of the war, he stayed in the army, with a marked interest in armoured units. He served in several military schools and joined the U.S. Army Command and General Staff School. Promoted to the grade of Major, this young visionary saw great potential in the airborne forces and, as from February 1940, he supervised the deployment of a Parachute Test Platoon at the Fort Benning infantry school. He was appointed commander of the HQ Provisional Parachute Group, which was officially activated on the 10th of March 1941. Promoted to the grade of Brigadier General on the 19th of April 1942, he became the very first commander at the Fort Benning jump school. In August 1942, Lee - now Major General- took command of the 101st U.S. Airborne Division, freshly formed at Camp Claiborne (Louisiana). He continued to prepare the unit up to its departure for Great Britain in September 1943. After suffering from a heart attack in February 1944, Major General Lee was replaced by Brigadier General Maxwell D. Taylor. He retired late 1944 and died at his home in Dunn barely four years later.

Lieutenant Colonel Lee, wearing the famous balloon suit and Riddell helmet, was not the kind of man to let the wool be pulled over his eyes. © NARA

During training, the cloth A-8 type flying helmet was replaced by a hard version that offered improved shock protection. It was a plastic helmet produced by the John T. Riddell Co., the designer and supplier of the American football helmet.
© Airborne Museum

The War Department launched a study on the 2nd of January 1940. A process which was accelerated by the German offensive in Europe in May - June, and the decisive role played by the *Fallschirmjäger* in operations. A Parachute Test Platoon was created on the 25th of June 1940. Of a total of 200 volunteers from the 29th Infantry Regiment, 48 were selected and placed under First Lieutenant William T. Ryder's command. This small unit was posted at the Lawson Army Airfield near Fort Benning. Thanks to military attachés in Germany and to the British forces, the Americans had obtained information on the *Fallschirmjäger* units; however, everything remained to be created on the Allied side. Jump and training techniques needed to be perfected, equipment designed, instruction manuals drafted, and the entire doctrine for the airborne army remained to be elaborated. Lee placed priority on autonomy and mobility. Each company integrated support units, so that it could operate and fight independently up to platoon level.

Training was organised in two phases. The first phase lasted 16 weeks and followed the men's initial training. Training focused on team work at all levels, by day and by night. The men were subjected to continuous races, physical and tactical instruction. They learned how to read maps, how to use a compass, were initiated into reconnaissance missions, and the handling of both explosives and available infantry weapons. For around ten days, they trained by jumping from the top of the two towers at the Safe Parachute Company in Highstown, of heights of 35 and 45 metres, whilst learning how to fold their parachutes. Their instructors were uncompromising as far as discipline was concerned, errors being punished by series of push-ups or pull-ups. Recruits tried their hand at jumping exercises on varying terrain, including stretches of water and woodlands. The second two week-long phase involved the entire battalion. The paras took part in extremely realistic manoeuvres, during which they faced a whole range of problems they were likely to encounter out in the field.

Front page of the Newsweek magazine's 9th June 1941 issue, showing the German parachutists who had wreaked terror in Greece and Crete. © Newsweek

Although promising, the airborne army's early days were no picnic. Back in Washington, Lee went to the utmost lengths to obtain the necessary material. The U.S. Army lacked in absolutely everything, and these new units were the worst off. Parachute production failed to keep up and new uniforms were quite simply nonexistent. Failing ideal conditions, the Test Platoon had no choice but to use B-1 suits and T-3 Air Force parachutes for jumps and training.

Lee regularly travelled to Fort Benning to monitor their progress. The eighth and last week was devoted to conducting the five jumps which offered the Parachute Test Platoon troops their parachutist qualification. On the 16th of August 1940, Ryder jumped from a plane, to make a soft landing at Lawson before an orchestra of VIPs. On the 16th of September 1940, the 1st Parachute Battalion became the first tactical parachute unit. A fortnight later, it became the 501st Parachute Infantry Battalion (PIB). On the 30th of April 1941, a Parachute School saw the day in Fort Benning. Due to the lack of army recruits, the 502nd PIB was activated on the 1st of July, by splitting the

This postcard illustrates one of the jumping towers at the Fort Benning Parachute School.
© Private collection

WILLIAM THOMAS RYDER (1913-1992)

When he graduated from the United States Military Academy at West Point in 1936, the officer William Thomas 'Bill' Ryder was considered as the first U.S. Army parachutist. Selected among 200 candidates, his results in the written exam placed him in command of the Test Parachute Platoon. Ryder created the Ryder's Death Ride, a 34 feet-high tower from which recruits trained at jumping. He also elaborated the U.S. Army's parachute training programme. On the 16th of August, together with 10 members of his platoon, First Lieutenant Ryder made the first jump from a Douglas C-33 plane in flight. The officer was the first to leave the plane, followed by Private William King. Promoted to the grade of Captain, he became Executive Officer (XO) of the Parachute School in May 1942 then, in April 1943, of the Airborne Command in Camp Mackall. On the 13th of July, he jumped over Sicily with Colonel James Gavin, the commander of the 505th PIR. In February 1944, Ryder was promoted to the grade of Colonel and sent to assist General MacArthur as Airborne Advisor. By the time he retired in 1966, he had become a military expert with the rank of Brigadier General. He was decorated with the Distinguished Service Medal, four Legions of Merit and two Bronze Star Medals. 'Bill' Ryder passed away in 1992 and is laid to rest in Arlington National Cemetery.

Ryder equipped with a T-4 parachute preparing to jump from the rear door of a C-33. The reserve parachute was attached to the harness by means of two carabiners. The officer is wearing boots with tightening straps at the feet.
© NARA

In 1942, Allen Pike published a 432-page illustrated book on the early days of the American airborne army.
© Private collection

first battalion in two. Then, the 503rd PIB was created on the 21st of August, and the 504th PIB on the 5th of October. Each battalion comprised 35 officers and 495 men.

After the Japanese attack on Pearl Harbor on the 7th of December 1941, the airborne army, considered as the elite, attracted existing young recruits, whilst fresh volunteers flocked to the U.S. Army recruitment offices. Despite their shared eagerness to be done with their nation's enemies, they still needed to successfully pass the medical selection phase, then to prove their worth during military training.

Paras from the 501st PIB proudly posing with their T-4 parachutes in front of a B-24 plane. Some are wearing leather gaiters on their U.S. Forest Service firemen's boots, to reinforce and protect their ankles. © NARA

Recruits from the 501st PIB training in all the movements they would need to reproduce after being dropped. © NARA

Eight Parachute Infantry Regiments (PIR), each comprised of three battalions, were created over the year of 1942, along with the Provisional Parachute Group and unified command - the Airborne Command - created on the 23rd of March. The fast growth in troop numbers - no longer a problem thanks to massive mobilisation - together with structuration of the army, enabled airborne divisions to be created. In theory, each regiment comprised 1,958 men. Given that the Fort Benning infrastructures were now insufficient, the Airborne Command moved to Fort Bragg, before setting up headquarters at Camp Mackall.

Comic strip published in 1941.
© Private collection

THE USE OF GLIDERS

Concurrently, the U.S. Army Air Corps experimented the use of gliders. For indeed, the plan was for 75% of future parachute division recruits to be transportable by air, which would require 6,000 pilots and a thousand gliders. Given the priority placed on the production of fighter and bomber planes, that of gliders was delayed. And recruiting their future pilots also proved complicated. By the 2nd of September 1941, 971 men had qualified.

The 550th Airborne Infantry Battalion (AIB), based in Fort Kobbe (Panama), and the 88th AIB from Fort Benning, were the first units to use the brand new CG4-A Waco gliders. The infantry troops were initially sent by twin-engined Douglas C-39 planes, the military version of the DC2. Over the autumn and the winter of 1941, the three Parachute Infantry Battalions took part in major manoeuvres in Louisiana which offered them an opportunity to demonstrate the scope of their skills.

The men were lined up on either side of the fuselage, their only safety device being a canvas waist belt. © NARA

This picture shows the rudimentary interior of the Waco glider, made of wood, canvas and metal tubes. © USAAF

This device enabled loads to be correctly adjusted within the glider cell, based on the number of men and the equipment on board. © Private collection

This picture shows the tow line through which a telephone wire enabled the glider crew to communicate with the tow plane.
© Rights reserved

THE WACO CG-4A GLIDER

Adopted in 1941, production of the Waco CG-4A - also known as the Hadrian glider - was launched the following year. The production lines of 16 companies worked on a round-the-clock basis. Hence, the Ford production plant in Kingsford (Michigan), produced a total of 4,190 gliders, whilst Waco Aircraft in Troy made 1,070. The glider's wood and metal superstructure was covered with canvas. Its articulated nose could be raised to allow vehicles to be loaded. It could transport 2 pilots and 13 men with their packs or one jeep, or one short 75mm howitzer. Small Clark Airborne CA-1 bulldozers could also be transported.

In contrast with the Horsa glider, the Waco's modest size meant it could land on small plots. © USAAF

A UNIFORM THAT WENT DOWN IN LEGEND

William P. Yarborough wearing the first prototype for the M41 jumpsuit. On his left, John M. Cole is wearing the balloon suit and the first version of buckled jump boots. © NARA

The creation of the American airborne army required for a whole range of specific equipment to be developed. From weapons to containers, via boots, personal equipment and helmets, everything needed to be designed in line with this new and somewhat complex form of military operation and with the practical doctrine of these paras who were required to operate behind the enemy lines for several days.

Uniforms needed to be both comfortable and lightweight, but also sufficiently airproof to ensure they did not become inflated during the jump. They also needed to include ample pockets to stock small material, food and extra ammunition.

The German parachutists (*Fallschirmjäger*) were the first to be equipped with specific gear, in particular their famous jump smocks (*Knochensack*) with large zipped pockets. The British copied it before designing their own Denison Smock camouflage jacket.

After wearing a number of poorly adapted or unsuitable overalls, the American paras were finally issued with specially designed outfits. The Infantry Board designed a jumpsuit which was tested by the 501st PIB over the winter of 1940-1941. Adopted by the spring, this famous balloon cloth jumpsuit was made from fabric originally used to make airships. Its baggy cut and difficult to reach zipped pockets, which also tended to catch elsewhere, made it impractical. For example its satin green colour reflected in the sunlight and proved very uncomfortable in the summer. Although it offered good wind protection, it was of a considerable disadvantage when nature came to call.

Captain William P. Yarborough from the 501st PIB, the man who drew the Jump Wings, designed a uniform comprised of trousers and a light khaki cotton poplin jacket that was both practical and of attractive design. The trousers were fitted with two pockets, closed with press studs and positioned on the side of the thighs so as not to get in the way of the parachute harness. It also had front and back pockets. The trousers were designed to be worn with braces and a belt, to ensure they stayed in place when the pockets were full.

The uniform jacket looked like a safari jacket with four flat pockets, two upper and two lower, all closed with press studs. It was fitted with a zip, a back comfort flap, a canvas waist belt and epaulettes. The chest pockets were asymmetrical to offer ease of access even when wearing jump gear. On the top of the collar, there was a small vertical pocket with two zips. It housed an M2 knife equipped with a detent to enable the paras to cut their straps and lines and to free themselves from their parachutes if required. The Infantry Board funded the production of prototypes by the Fort Benning tailor.

Although of attractive design, the M-1941 uniform proved to present several drawbacks when worn.

The pockets were too small and the press studs (one per pocket) were insufficient. A new version, referred to as the M-1942 was ready for use by December 1941. The trousers were fitted with bellows cargo pockets, closed by means of two press studs, and sufficiently large to contain a complete K ration (three packages). The same applied to the jacket pockets. However, the uniform had its failings. The light khaki colour was ill-adapted to certain theatres of operation, in Europe in particular. Furthermore, as it was intensively used both in training and in combat, early wear and tear was observed at the elbows and knees, poplin not being a particularly robust fabric. The seams of the heavily burdened pockets offered poor resistance to shocks upon parachute opening. This uniform nevertheless remained the paras' favourite up to the end of the war.

The cut of the M-42 jump jacket with its four bellows pockets was extremely modern at the time and offered paratroopers great ease of movement. This example is almost brand new and is fitted with Crown & Serval zips. © Private collection

These parachutists have just landed and are wearing the M-42 uniform. Note the white canopy of their T-5 parachutes. The man in the foreground is covering his fellow paras with his PM Thompson gun before even freeing himself from his harnass. © Getty images

THE PARA'S GEAR

The T-5 parachute

The Test Platoon and the 501st PIB used T-3 training parachutes, then T-4 static line parachutes developed by Irvin Air Chute, and equipped with white silk canopies that were specially designed in the summer of 1940. At this stage, Wright Field engineers were already working on the following model, the T-5. On the 23rd of April 1941, three prototypes including fast harness closing systems were sent to Fort Benning to be tested. The initially selected Quick Release System (similar to the British X Type) was finally rejected following the accidental opening of a harness during flight, leading to the death of a parachutist. The chosen solution was in the form of a harness closed by means of three carabiners and with a chest belt. The T-5 was adopted on the 13th of June 1941, to become the first individual automatic release parachute with an independent 'reserve' parachute with manually activated opening. The back parachute had a 52m^2 28-panel canopy, whereas the chest parachute canopy was comprised of 24 panels for a surface of 45m^2. The silk canopies were replaced with more resistant nylon ones. The back parachutes were made of white or camouflaged canopies as from 1944.

Compared to the previous model, the T-5 parachute used in Normandy was equipped with khaki coloured straps, harness and static line. A ring stitched to the front of the harness enabled a Griswold protection case, housing a Garand M1 rifle, to be attached.
© Mémorial de Caen collection/Photo C. Prime

M2 helmet with signs of camouflaging, which was commonplace among troops from the 82nd Airborne Division since the Sicily campaign. © Airborne Museum

The M2 helmet

In June 1941, the U.S. Army adopted a new one-size heavy helmet, the M1, inside which a cardboard or compressed fibre liner was placed. However, the M1 helmet proved to be poorly suited for use by parachutists. Indeed, due to the jolt provoked by opening the canopy, these two helmet features became separated. To solve this problem, a specific helmet - the M2 - was produced. The steel helmet chin straps were extended so they could be attached to the liner via a stud press system and the jugular fixation loops were rounded so that they could freely move forwards and backwards. On either side of the liner, reverse A-shaped straps were attached to a leather chin strap. With use, the salient semi-circular fixation loops tended to break. Many M2 helmets bore the signs of makeshift repairs. The M2 heavy helmet was gradually replaced by the standard M1 model, followed by the M1C with mobile straps.

Advert published by Nash Kelvinator, a company which produced plane engines, in particular.
© Private collection

Jump Wings

On the 3rd of March 1941, Captain Yarborough from the 501st PIB was entrusted with the mission of drawing the parachutists' insignia, referred to as Jump Wings. His project was approved by the War Department on the 10th. The same officer also created the Senior and Master Parachutist Badges. This cautious man took care to protect his creations with a patent.

Parachutist's jump badge made by Sterling Modele. It was awarded to soldiers after five qualifying jumps. A star was added for each operational jump.
© Private collection

Boots, Parachute Jumper

Landing on the ground was the moment when the paras were most likely to hurt themselves, particularly their ankles. The Infantry Board, in charge of designing new equipment, studied the laced boots worn by German parachutists and those of the firemen from the U.S. Forest Service, equipped with a tightening strap at the top of the foot. Captain Yarborough designed several prototypes, which were tested by the 501st PIB, and progressively improved. A final Boots, Parachute Jumper model was adopted in August 1942. They were fitted with two-part rubber soles. The heals were bevelled and hollow to create a shock-absorbing effect. The high ankle shafts with 11 to 13 hook eylets were reinforced at the back and the toes were capped. Whilst Corcoran was the most widely known manufacturer, Herman Shoes, International Shoe and Red Wing Shoe also contributed.

Pair of jump boots that once belonged to PVT (Private) Kenneth E. Russell, who fell on the church roof in Sainte-Mère.
© Airborne Museum

THE BIRTH OF THE ALL AMERICANS

The image of the parachutist was several times reproduced on billboards, magazine and comic covers, for this elite force of a brand new kind was the very symbol of courage, excellence and tenacity. © NARA

The shoulder insignia of the 82nd U.S. Infantry Division remained the same, even after the unit became airborne. The word Airborne was simply added to the top of the badge. © Private collection

The 82nd U.S. Infantry Division was reactivated on the 25th of March 1942 at Camp Claiborne. The unit was of a brand new kind, for it comprised 2,000 officers, NCOs and specialists from the 9th U.S. Infantry Division, together with 16,000 new recruits or drafted troops. It was commanded by Major General Omar Bradley, with Brigadier General Matthew Ridgway second-in-command. All staff followed a 17-week infantry training programme. In theory, the unit was to take part in the landing operation on the French coast in April 1943 (operation Round Up).

On the 26th of June, Ridgway took command of the division following his superior's posting elsewhere. After having been informed of the unit's transformation into a motorised infantry division, he discovered that the 82nd U.S. Infantry Division was, in fact, to become the U.S. Army's first airborne division - given its excellent level of military training, high troop morale and quality command.

The 82nd ID officially became an airborne unit on the 15th of August 1942, concurrent to its sister unit, the 101st Airborne Division, commanded by General Lee. Despite their scepticism regarding this new force, around 4,500 men requested to be drafted. Any men inapt for parachute jumping were transferred, whilst the future glidermen were sent to the U.S. Army Air Forces (USAAF) base in Laurinburg-Maxton. In October 1942, the

Paras in training. They absolutely needed to stay in tip-top form to accomplish their future missions. © NARA

Jumping into the void from the top of the Fort Benning jump towers required considerable self-control and composure. © NARA

Jumpmasters making one last check on the paras' equipment before the jump. © NARA

As we neared our time to leave, on the way to war, I had an exercise that required them to leave our barracks area at 7pm, and march all night to an area near the town of Cottonwood, Alabama, a march about 23 miles. There, we maneouvred all day and in effect we seized and held an airhead. We broke up the exercise about 8pm and started the troopers back by another route through dense pine forest, by way of backwoods roads. About 11pm, we went into bivouac. After about one hour's sleep, the troopers were awakened to resume the march. In 36 hours, the regiment had marched well over 50 miles, manoeuvred and seized an airhead and defended it from counter-attack while carrying full combat loads and living off reserve rations.

Colonel James Gavin, 505th PIR

82nd Airborne Division, essentially comprised of the 504th PIR, the 325th GIR, the 376th PFAB and the 307th AEB, left Louisiana and took up its new quarters at Fort Bragg in North Carolina.

Colonel James Gavin's 505th PIR, which joined the 82nd Airborne Division on the 10th of February 1943, was sent to Camp Billy Mitchell in Alabama.

Over long months, the recruits who had volunteered to join the force were subjected to extremely strenuous physical training before being sent to Fort Benning for their four-week period of jump training:
- phase A: physical training;
- phase B: folding and jump exercises from 11 metre-high towers;
- phase C: jump exercises from 76 metre-high towers;
- phase D: five qualifying jumps.

Concurrently, they took part in intensive combat exercise, and trained in handling weapons and equipment depending on their specialities. Their instructors strove to reinforce their physical condition, readily pushing them beyond their limits, in particular during orienteering exercises by night, equipped with their complete combat gear. Competition between units, together with sports events, reinforced the esprit de corps. The paras earned themselves a reputation as tough guys.

Tree trunk throwing was a test of strength and cohesion. © NARA

The paras from the 505th PIR preparing to board. They are all wearing a nationality armband on their right arm, a habit that they kept whilst in Normandy. © NARA

CHAPTER 2

EARLY COMBAT

SICILY

In the month of February 1943, Ridgway and his military staff were informed of the division's transfer to North Africa, scheduled for the month of May. They absolutely needed to complete their training before setting sail. The troopers and gliders landed in Casablanca to join the Moroccan region of Oujda, cramped aboard goods wagons. After their exhausting journey, they set up their tents in the vicinity of Marnia on the 24th of May 1943. Since it boasted insufficient Waco gliders, the 82nd AB integrated the 505th PIR and the 456th FAB.

Ridgway immediately summoned Colonel James Gavin, nicknamed 'Slim Jim' to inform him that his 505th PIR was to be the first regiment engaged in Sicily. The 3rd Battalion from the 504th PIR, the 456th Parachute Field Artillery Battalion (PFAB), an engineer unit, a medical detachment and a signal unit were to join the regiment to collectively form a Parachute Regimental Combat Team (PRCT) a sufficiently powerful tactical unit to accomplish the mission it had been entrusted with. A second PRCT was formed around the 504th PIR.

Pending their engagement, the American paras were accommodated in tents, in intense heat. They experimented some novel and somewhat surprising techniques. Indeed, they tried dropping mules equipped with parachutes, for they could well prove useful for bringing supplies to units in some of Sicily's rugged landscapes. Sadly, upon landing, they broke their legs and had to be put down.

A trooper attaching the harness of his T-5 parachute. The white straps indicate that this one is the first model.
© NARA

On the Mediterranean front, the American paras preferred using the compact training gas masks. © Private collection

A month after the operation's launch, Gavin, two battalion commanders and two pilots from the 52nd Trooper Carrier Wing headed to Malta where they boarded the five De Havilland Mosquito planes that would fly them over Gela in reconnaissance of the flight path and the landing zone. They chose to operate by night, for the moon was in the same phase as it would be on the night of the assault. However, prime targets for the Flak, the planes were forced to retreat rapidly, putting a premature end to their reconnaissance mission. At dawn on the 16th of June, the All Americans left Oudja to head for a base located 50 kilometres from the Tunisian town of Kairouan.

Gliders opening the cockpit of a Waco to load a 75mm Pack Howitzer M8. © NARA

Two paras installing an A-5 canvas container in the space provided for it under the wing of a C-47. © NARA

On the night of the 9th to the 10th of July, under Gavin's command, the 3,405 men from the 505th PRCT jumped near Gela in Sicily (operation Husky I). Their initial mission was to pave the way for the 1st U.S. Infantry Division. To ensure top security, the soldiers could not be informed of their destination prior to take-off. Each of them had been issued with a small piece of paper upon which the following message was written, 'Soldiers of the 505th Combat Team, tonight you embark upon a combat mission for which our people and the free people of the world have been waiting for two years. You will spearhead the landing of the American Force upon the island of Sicily. You have been given the means to do the job and you are backed by the largest assemblage of air power in the world's history. The eyes of the world are upon you. The hopes and the prayers of every American go with you.'

The first engagement got off to a bad start. Of the 226 transport planes involved, 8 were reported missing and 3 returned to base without dropping their sticks. The crews lacked in experience and certain sticks were dropped at an altitude of 100 metres rather than the required 250 metres. Only 15% of all troops landed in or close to their planned drop zones due to poor visibility and strong winds. The vast majority of sticks were dispersed in zones over 50km from their targets. Trained to engage in combat whatever the circumstances, the paras managed to reunite. They cut telephone lines, attacked targets of opportunity, enemy patrols and cleared the defensive positions that happened to be in their sector of operation. Fourteen troopers neutralised several casemates, capturing over 250 Italian soldiers.

Once equipped, the men boarded their aircraft. Sometimes, a helping hand from ground staff proved necessary. © NARA

Once on board, these two paras have dozed off. But their crossing will be short-lived.
© R. Capa/Magnum

The 82nd Airborne Division created sufficient havoc to slow down the arrival of enemy reinforcements and to allow the 45th U.S. Infantry Division to break through from the beach. However, the imminent arrival of the powerful *Hermann Göring Fallschirmpanzer Division* took them by surprise, for the paras were insufficiently equipped in weapons to effectively counter these armoured units, in particular the new *Tiger IE* heavy tanks facing which their bazookas proved futile. Covered by three howitzers and two antitank guns, Colonel Gavin and some 300 men nevertheless stopped a German armoured attack on the Biazza Ridge. The *Panzers* were within 50 metres of the regiment's command post. However, the situation was soon to be under control, thanks to the intervention of 45th U.S. Infantry Division 155mm howitzers and navy guns.

The soldiers who took part in operation Husky were issued with a small guide book to learn the local habits and customs, in order to avoid blunders. © Private collection

Major General Ridgway (Two Stars) on the Sicilian front. Just like his paras, his M2 helmet bears the highly characteristic camouflage. He kept it throughout his career. Today, it is among the exhibits at the D-Day Experience visitor centre in Saint-Côme-du-Mont. © NARA

MATTHEW BUNKER RIDGWAY (1895-1993)

Son of an artillery officer, born in Fort Monroe (Virginia), he graduated from West Point in 1917. He returned to this prestigious academy the following year to teach Spanish. In 1925, First Lieutenant Ridgway was posted to China, then to Nicaragua two years later. Appointed military adviser to the Governor General of the Philippines in 1930, he integrated the Fort Leavenworth Command and General Staff School (Kansas) in 1935, then the Army War College at Carlisle Barracks two years later. The officer made quite an impression on General George Marshall, before integrating the War Plans Division in Washington DC. He was promoted to the rank of Major General in August 1942 and took command of the 82nd U.S. Airborne Division until September 1944, the date of his appointment in command of the XVIII Airborne Corps. He led his troops to the centre of Germany. After Japan's capitulation, Ridgway was named Lieutenant General and took command of the American military forces in the Mediterranean, before being appointed U.S. representative at the United Nations Military Staff Committee. In 1948, he commanded the American forces based in the Carribean then, the following year, he was placed under the U.S. Army Chief of Staff, General Lawton J. Collins' command. In 1950, he took command of the Eighth U.S. Army, deployed in Korea, to become military governor of Japan after MacArthur was removed from command. In 1952, Matthew Ridgway replaced Eisenhower as Supreme Allied Commander Europe and prepared the transition towards NATO. In August 1953, he was appointed Chief of Staff of the U.S. Army. He retired from active service on the 30th of June 1955. Matthew Ridgway died on the 26th of July 1993 in Pittsburgh, at the age of 98 years. He is laid to rest in Arlington National Cemetery.

It took several days to reunite the All Americans, who were scattered over a vast sector. Exhausted men cramped in the back of a GMC truck. © NARA

The men from the 2/505 PIR's HQ Company entered the port of Naples on the 2nd of October 1943. © NARA

The situation remained very tense for the paras. Lieutenant Colonel Arthur Gorham, commander of the 1/505 PIR took up position on a height by the Comico airfield with a handful of his men. On the 11th, ten German tanks and an infantry battalion launched an assault on their position. Gorham stood up amidst the gunfire and harangued his men, who were all lying flat on the ground. The officer seized a bazooka, destroyed a *Panzer* whilst commanding his paras' gunfure until the attack was finally thrust back. The following day, he reiterated, but was killed by gunfire from the Tiger tank he was aiming at. He was posthumously awarded the Distinguished Service Cross.

The two other 504th PRCT battalions, commanded by Colonel Reuben 'Rube' Tucker, the 376th PFAB, the 307th Airborne Engineer Battalion's C Company and support units left Kairouan on the 11th of July (operation Husky II) to be dropped near the Farello airfield. Unfortunately, the servers of the anti-aircraft defence guns, together with those of the 45th U.S. Infantry Division, mistakenly opened fire on the 144 twin-engined planes from the 316th Transport Carrier Group (TCG) as they flew above them. Twenty-three planes were shot down, 37 seriously damaged and 318 paratroopers were killed, wounded or unaccounted for. Brigadier General Charles Leslie 'Bull' Keerans, second-in-command of the division and who had come as a simple observer, was declared MIA (Missing in Action).

The All Americans then accompanied the progression made by the Seventh U.S. Army, commanded by Lieutenant General Patton, who was eager to preserve this elite troop. However, such preservation did not prevent certain recruits from distinguishing themselves, in particular in the Tumminello Pass and in Trapani. On the 16th of July, with 1,424 soldiers unaccounted for, Ridway was in command of 3,883 out of 5,307 men. He nevertheless sealed the surrender of the troops defending Palermo on the 23rd of July.

The paras took several white arms with them, but also American knuckle dusters. A lesser-known fact is that the All Americans were the first to use crickets or clickers to recognise each other in Sicily. This one was found in Normandy in a sector where the 82nd U.S. Airborne Division was present.
© Private collection

Despite the division getting off to a laborious start, the U.S. Paras had largely facilitated the breakthrough to the island's inland areas for sealanded units. They had also demonstrated their combativity in all circumstances. Many lessons were learned from the operation, in particular on the use of pathfinders to mark out drop zones (DZ).

Once back in North Africa, new recruits were integrated and training resumed. The 3/504th PIR and the 325th GIR were sent to Bizerte to form an amphibious assault unit with the rangers. The high command was already hard at work on an operation aimed at giving them a foothold in Southern Italy. General Montgomery's Eighth Army was to land in the Reggio sector in Calabria (operation Baytown), whilst the Fifth United States Army's key target was Salerno (operation Avalanche).

An airborne assault was scheduled to take control of the Sorrento ridge overlooking the beaches, where the U.S. troops were to land. The 82nd U.S. Airborne Division's superior officers were informed of their mission on the 1st of August. The military staff changed the initial plan to finally opt for two operations. The first, Giant One, was aimed at taking control of the coastal plain leading to the city of Naples, together with the bridges over the River Volturno, in order to block any German counter-attacks. Giant Two was an amphibious and airborne assault aimed at capturing Rome. On the 20th of August, the unit reached Sicily to prepare their forthcoming operational jump. Once in Italy, confusion was rife and the nation's occupation by the German army meant that both operations were to be cancelled.

A C-53 Skytrooper returning from Sicily. It is recognisable thanks to the absence of the cargo door. The tip of its left wing suffered damage during a collision. © NARA

DOUGLAS C-47 SKYTRAIN AND C-53 SKYTROOPER PLANES

In 1940, the U.S. Air Force passed an order for a military version of the Douglas DC3 twin-engined plane. Over and above the C-47 Skytrain's four or five crew members, the plane could transport 18 passengers or 4 tonnes of freight thanks to its reinforced structure. Containers suitable for airdrops were attached under the wings. The plane could reach a maximum speed of 370 km/h with a flying autonomy of 2,400km. The C-53 Skytrooper- a version exclusively reserved for troop transport- was also developed. Although very similar to the Skytrain, it was equipped neither with a reinforced loading floor nor a cargo door.

Gavin briefing the men from his stick. Their faces have already been camouflaged but their M36 musette bags are still half empty. © NARA

SALERNO

On the 4th of September 1943, Lieutenant General Mark Clark's Fifth Army landed in the bay of Salerno to the south of Naples, during operation Avalanche. *Generalfeldmarschall Kesselring* reunited his forces and launched a violent counter-attack on the 13th of September. The German tanks progressed along the banks of the River Sele, giving the 36th and 45th U.S. Infantry Divisions a hard time. The situation became critical for Clark, who had no reserve troops to engage. Lieutenant Colonel Yarborough, his Airborne Advisor, suggested he engage the 82nd Airborne Division, at the time based in Licata in Sicily.

Ridgway gave the go ahead. The 51st and 52nd Troop Carrier Wings, in charge of transporting the paras, were informed at 1.30pm the same day. Three planes took off at 7.30pm with 50 pathfinders on board. For safety reasons, the Allied anti-aircraft defence was ordered to remain silent. The pathfinders marked out the DZ near Paestum using Eureka transponders and Aldis lamps. A little later,

Lieutenant Colonel Charles W. Kouns was in command of the 3/504 PIR. The battalion only comprised 59 men. It took the unit 10 days to reunite and Kouns, who was captured on the 13th of July, spent the rest of the war in an *oflag*. © NARA

Major William P. Yarborough took part in the first American manoeuvres of operation Torch, along with the 509th PIB. Appointed as commander of the 2/504 PIR in March 1943, he was promoted to the rank of Lieutenant Colonel in May. He took command of the 509th PIB prior to the liberation of Naples. © NARA

Troopers from the 504th PIR reporting back to their lieutenant on their return from a patrol. © NARA

Paras demining the Volturno slopes. © NARA

1,300 men from the 1/504 and 2/504 PIR, together with two platoons from the 307th AEB, followed the next day by 2,100 505th PIR paras, were dropped over the bridgehead.

Three 3/504 PIR companies and a share of the 325th GIR were sent by sea on the 11th of September. Tucker and his men bitterly defended the heights overlooking Altavilla. The 504th PIR forced back several counter-attacks, obliging the Germans to retreat and saving the bridgehead in the process. The entire unit was awarded the Distinguished Service Cross for this great feat of arms.

Over the following days, the 82nd Airborne Division advanced along the coastal plain, on the Fifth U.S. Army's left flank. The All Americans were the first to enter Naples on the 1st of October 1943. Major Ed 'Cannonball' Kraus from the 3/505 PIR hoisted the Star-Spangled Banner on top of the Italian post office building. A few days later, the 505th PIR took the bridges over the canals in the town of Arnone, before being subjected to a counter-attack that forced the regiment into retreat.

A vast share of the 82nd Airborne Division then left the Mediterranean front to head to Great Britain to prepare for a landing operation on the French coast. The 504th PIR, with reinforcements from the 376th and 456th PFABs, stayed put. The regiment engaged in fierce combat to save the Anzio bridgehead (operation Shingle) from the 22nd of January to the 23rd of March 1944. One German officer jotted down in his diary, 'Enemy patrols in baggy pants are 100 metres from my command post. We know neither who they are, nor where they come from. It seems the black devils (the soldiers had blackened their faces for patrol missions) are everywhere.' The Devils in Baggy Pants earned themselves quite a reputation.

M3 trench knife and its M6 leather case, made by Viner Bros in 1943.
© Airborne Museum

The parachutist's complete weaponry. Along with his Garand rifle and automatic pistol, he was also issued with a trench knife, four hand grenades and six 60mm mortar shells. © NARA

AIRBORNE TROOP WEAPONS

The paras were issued with the same individual weapons as the U.S. Army infantrymen, i.e. Garand M1 rifles, M1928 Thomson submachine guns, M3 Grease Guns, and M1A1 folding stock carbines. Independently of their rank or speciality, they all carried a Colt 1911A1 automatic pistol. They were also issued with blade weapons for hand-to-hand combat. The M3 trench knife was used in association with personal blades. Extensive stocks of Mk2 A1 defensive grenades were also issued. In Normandy, this arsenal was completed with Gammon No. 82 grenades which exploded on impact, and with Hawkins No. 75 mines, which proved effective against vehicles. To counter the enemy tanks, the paras had a 60mm M1 bazooka which was far from offering optimal efficiency. The troopers and glidermen offered support fire with BARs (Browning Automatic Rifles), .30 calibre M1919 machine guns and 60 or 80mm M1 mortars. It was only when the gliders arrived that they also recovered 57mm antitank guns and 75mm Pack Howitzers M8. Hence, the 82nd Airborne Division had at its disposal one airborne, two airlanded and three artillery battalions. Each battalion was equipped with three batteries formed of four 75mm howitzers. Anti-aircraft batteries were equipped with .50 calibre machine guns on mounts.

THE ALL AMERICANS IN GREAT BRITAIN

The British Prime Minister Winston Churchill and General Eisenhower inspecting an airborne unit (101st U.S. Airborne). © NARA

Paras advancing through a dummy village somewhere in England. © NARA

The bulk of the 82nd Airborne Division left Italy to head for Great Britain. A whole range of changes were enforced. Colonel Gavin, promoted to the rank of Brigadier General, was appointed second-in-command of the division in December 1943. Lieutenant Colonel Herbert Batcheller replaced him in charge of the 505th PIR.

On the 18th of November, the regiment boarded *USS Frederick Funston* to sail to Belfast where they docked on the 9th of December. The 505th PIR set up quarters in Cookstown up to the 13th of February, the date it crossed the Irish Sea on its way to Camp Quorn in Leicestershire. Lieutenant Colonel William Ekman became his new chief on the 22nd of March 1944.

On the 28th of December 1943, the 508th PIR boarded the troop transport ship *USAT James Parker*. Twelve days later, the parachutists landed in the port of Belfast. The 507th PIR had already been hard at work in Ireland for several weeks. The two regiments were attached to the 82nd Airborne Division on the 14th of January 1944.

C-47s in arrow formation dropping their sticks over the English countryside. The concentration of parachute canopies offer proof of the exercise's success. © NARA

Colonel George V. Millett Jr.'s 507th PIR in turn headed for Nottingham, England in March 1944. The 508th PIR continued its training over the following two months in Cromore, on the island of Lewis on the west coast of Scotland. The unit then headed for Glasgow, to take a train to Wollaton Park in Nottinghamshire on the 13th of March.

Based in Portglenone forest since their arrival in Northern Ireland on the 9th of December, the 325th GIR sailed to Liverpool before heading for Camp March Hare in the vicinity of Leicester on the 15th of February. The regiment was reinforced upon the arrival of the 401st GIR's 3rd Battalion.

The men were accommodated in large pyramid-shaped tents equipped with a stove and a cement floor. Upon its arrival, the unit integrated new recruits and resumed training in the heart of the West Midlands countryside. In preparation for D-Day, they made successive jumps, marches and tactical exercises, by day and by night.

THE 504TH PIR, THE GREAT ABSENTEE

The 504th PIR left the Italian peninsula aboard the *RMMV Capetown Castle* liner to land in Liverpool on the 22nd of April 1944. The combat in Italy had bled them dry. More than 1,100 men had been killed, wounded or were unaccounted for. Two battalion chiefs were among the victims. Gavin was keen for the regiment to take part in the invasion by recruiting from the 507th and 508th PIRs; however Ridgway refused, considering that the unit was already considerably weakened. Only twenty volunteers actually participated in operaton Neptune as pathfinders in other units, or as General Gavin's bodyguards.

We went into a tent city and set up camp there. There we were to practice our jumping, night jumping, and a lot of exercise to get us back in physical shape. After three or four day jumps, we started making night jumps and found that the winds were too much in Ireland to jump at night. We were landing in farmhouses and farmers' fields. A lot of these villagers weren't told the Americans were going to land that particular night, and a lot of boys were out there under siege by the farmers standing there with pitchforks trying to defend their farms. Consequently, the higher-ups decided this was a bad deal, so we were taken from Belfast by ship to Nottingham, England.

Private Dick Johnson, HQ Company, 1/507 PIR

To perfect their reflexes, the airborne troops conducted massive airdrops, both by day and by night, during their posting in Great Britain. © NARA

COMPOSITION OF THE 82ND AIRBORNE DIVISION (1944)

Integrated within Major General Collins' VII U.S. Corps, the division was comprised of three parachute regiments and one airlanded infantry regiment, together with support units. Its total of 11,979 men, all organs and units combined, were equipped with around 300 jeeps, 100 trucks, 100 mortars, 36 75mm howitzers and 57mm antitank guns.

The 61st Transport Carrier Wings' C-47 R-292641 - baptised Turf and Sport Special - transported the paras from the 508th PIR's E Company. On board, PFC (Private First Class) Joe Morettini was wounded on the 4th of July 1944 during the attack on Hill 195. This picture of the plane was taken during operation Market Garden. © USAAF

CHAPTER 3

BY THE LONGEST NIGHT

Aerial photograph of Sainte-Mère-Église. © NARA

A NEW MISSION: NORMANDY

As the great day approached, the officers notified their subordinates of the latest available information, reiterating the important elements of their missions during short daily briefings. © NARA

The initial plan devised by the Chief of Staff to Supreme Allied Commander (COSSAC), commanded by Lieutenant General Frederick E. Morgan, was considerably altered by the Supreme Headquarters Allied Expeditionary Force (SHAEF), by extending the assault sector on either of its extremities. Two new beaches were added to the three existing ones: Sword to the east and Utah to the west. The Allied high command decided to precede the amphibious landing operation by an airborne attack. The 6th British Airborne Division, entrusted with covering the east flank, was to capture the bridges over the Orne and the canal from Caen to the sea, and to neutralise the German artillery battery in Merville. To the west, the 82nd and 101st U.S. Airborne Divisions were to jump over the Cotentin peninsula to pave the way for the units coming from Utah Beach.

The plan was to drop the 82nd Airborne Division to the west of Saint-Sauveur-le-Vicomte, in order to cut the peninsula above the line of marshes and to block the German forces, hence obliging them to converge towards Utah. However, early May, the Allied intelligence department was informed of the arrival of the *91. Luftlande Infanterie Division (91. LLD)* in the sector around Saint-Sauveur-le-Vicomte, the 82nd Airborne Division's initial target. The *6. Fallschirmjäger Regiment (FJR6)*, posted around La Haye-du-Puits, had come to reinforce the German positions, along with a tank instruction battalion, the *Panzer-Ersatz-und Ausbildungs-Abteilung 100.*

Air Chief Marshal Leigh Mallory notified the Allied command that losses among airborne troops could be in the region of 70%. Eisenhower decided to maintain the operation, for postponing it would seriously compromise overall chances of success. However, the site where the All Americans were supposed to engage was modified a few days prior to the operation's launch. They were dropped on either bank of the River Merderet.

The mission entrusted to the 505th PIR consisted in capturing the village of Sainte-Mère-Église and taking control of the bridges over the River Merderet. Control of the communication nerve centre, located on the RN13 trunk road between Caen and Cherbourg, was to enable the Allies to prevent German reinforcements from coming from Cherbourg. The 507th and 508th PIR were to be dropped respectively in the sectors of Amfreville and Picauville to offer support to the 505th PIR and to either take control of, or destroy the bridges over the River Douve, in prevision of future operations further westwards in Cotentin. The 325th GIR and support units were to arrive in several waves from the 6th to the 8th of June. Just like in Italy, the last airlanded elements would be landed on the beaches. A Task Force commanded by Colonel Edson Raff was entrusted with the mission of heading straight for Sainte-Mère-Église. It was comprised of a company from the 325th GIR, a tank company from the 746th Tank Battalion, a battery from the 319th GFAB and a platoon from the 4th Reconnaissance Squadron. The change in plans did not for as much modify the unit's engagement in three phases. On the 26th of May, the SHAEF unveiled the final plans for operation Overlord. The 82nd Airborne Division was to be deployed in three successive waves. The airdrop plans were ready. Orders had been given. Regiment and battalion chiefs were officially informed of the scope and content of their respective missions. They were issued with 1/5,000 scale maps of the operation sector.

	Force A	Force B	Force C
Commander	Brigadier General Gavin	Major General Ridgway	Brigadier General Howell
Force	6,420 men	3,773 men	1,712 men
Engagement	6 June 1944	6-7 June 1944	6 June
Engagement mode	Parachute drop	Glider	Amphibious

A group of 82nd Airborne Division paras posing for posterity. One of them has a Bell & Howell camera. © NARA

TROOP CARRIER GROUPS

Shoulder badge worn by staff from the Transport Carrier Groups in charge of transporting airborne forces. © NARA

The IX Troop Carrier Command (TCC) was activated on the 16th of October 1943, five days prior to the start of its transfer to Great Britain. Its role was to transport airborne units to their respective zones. The command's headquarters were set up in the Royal Air Force base in Cottesmore, before moving to Grantham. A total of fifteen airfields were chosen to welcome the 50th, 52nd and 53rd Troop Carrier Wings (TCW), which were successively brought in from Sicily and the United States.

A C-47 Skytrain crew during a final check before setting off on a mission. They were all issued with M4 and T-3 anti-Flak helmets together with armoured chest plates to protect them against Flak fire. © NARA

Each site welcomed a group of four Troop Carrier Squadrons, i.e. forty C-47s and as many gliders.

The crews of the 50th and 52nd TCWs trained intensively with airborne units in preparation for operation Neptune. Several mass drops were conducted by night up to April 1944. The 53rd TCW, which had arrived from the United States the previous month, was totally inexperienced compared to the two other units which had operated in the Mediterranean. Crew training continued up to May. These groups were to convoy the gliders. On the 1st of June, the IX TCC lined up its 1,200 C-47 planes, 1,400 Waco and Horsa gliders and 1,900 crew members.

Inside a C-47 cockpit. © Rights reserved

Planes belonging to the 439th Troop Carrier Group meticulously lined up on the runway at the Upottery base. Their future mission would be to take the men from the 101st U.S. Airborne to their destinations. © NARA

The airlanded infantry preparing to board. Althought this force lacked recognition, its role was crucial, and without its help, the paras would most likely never have reached their targets nor maintained their positions. © NARA

THE GLIDERMEN

The American military planners hoped to deploy the gliders at the start of the operation to quickly obtain a concentration of units on the ground. However, the discovery of vast areas that had been flooded and covered with wooden stakes by the Germans, together with the great risks involved in the massive use of gliders, led to the decision not to engage all gliders by night. The accidents that occurred during simple exercises revealed the great risks that would be taken by commanders, should conditions for engagement fail to be ideal.

Landing Zone W (LZ W), in 'Les Forges', a locality two kilometres to the south-east of Sainte-Mère-Église was chosen to land gliders. Drop Zone O (DZ O) was also capable of welcoming them.

At 4am on the 6th of June, fifty-two CG-4 Waco gliders were to transport 220 men, 27 vehicles, 16 57mm antitank guns and 10 tonnes of ammunition and material. This first glider landing operation, codenamed Detroit, was initially scheduled to take place at dawn; however, it was advanced by two hours, to benefit from the cover of the night.

USAAF shoulder badge. The gliders engaged in Normandy wore their divisions' insignia. © NARA

DELAYED RECONNAISSANCE

Whilst the task facing the glidermen was just as perilous and as vital as that of the paratroopers, they enjoyed less consideration and lower pay. Paratroop officers ware awarded a bonus of $100 per month, and ordinary paras $50 when they took part in wartime missions. Their fellow soldiers in glider units received no extra pay. What's more, the latter were not authorised to wear qualification insignia, and were issued neither with a specific uniform, nor even with jump boots. Much to their dismay, apart from the division insignia worn on the left shoulder, nothing distinguished them from ordinary soldiers. It was only in July 1944 that they were allowed to wear Glider Wings and to finally benefit from a risk-related bonus.

Loading a Waco glider was not a matter of improvisation. Incorrect load distribution or insufficient securing of vehicles and artillery pieces could have disastrous consequences. © NARA

I'd give a month's wages for the son-of-a-bitch from Washington, who decided that to crash land in one of these canvas coffins wasn't dangerous, to come with us just once.

Anonymous

Mission Elmira mobilised much more impressive means in the form of 36 Waco gliders, 130 Horsa gliders, all towed by 176 C-47 planes, arriving in four waves, from 9pm to 11pm on the evening of the 6th of June. They transported the anti-aircraft defence, field artillery and antitank units, a share of the division's military staff, the reconnaissance platoon and a medical outpost.

As from 6am on the 7th of June, supplies were dropped by parachute (mission Freeport).

A fleet comprised of 107 Waco and 43 Horsa gliders transporting the 325th GIR and some reinforcements landed at 7 and 9am (missions Galveston and Hackensack). Due to insufficient gliders, several hundred glider troops were transported by boat and landed on Utah Beach.

Pulleys found on the wreck of a Waco glider.
© Private collection

PATHFINDERS

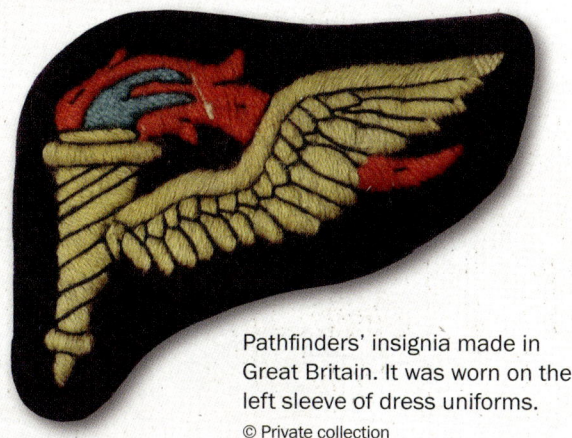

Pathfinders' insignia made in Great Britain. It was worn on the left sleeve of dress uniforms.
© Private collection

The drop errors experienced in Sicily had led the airborne troops to reconsider their engagement tactics, calling upon pathfinders to mark out drop zones and glider landing zones, in order to facilitate target location from the air and to prevent too many men or their craft from going astray.

A special group of 20 planes based in North Witham had been created within the 52nd TCW to accompany the pathfinders from the 82nd and 101st Airborne Divisions. Lieutenant Colonel Joel Crouch's crews offered the paras a great deal of precious advice, so that they could efficiently guide the bulk of the airborne forces towards their drop and landing zones. The same pathfinders would take them to Normandy.

Each parachute regiment was allocated three teams of pathfinders, recruited on a voluntary basis, including in the ranks of the 504th PIR. Each team comprised a Lieutenant and his second-in-command, two Eureka operators and their assistants, a section chief for the Holophane lamps, seven paras in charge of installing them - two lamps per para - and four to six men in charge of ensuring zone security.

The teams were also all equipped with two Eureka AN/PPN-1A transponders which, once lit, sent radio pulses to the Rebecca APN-2 (SCR-729) transceivers installed under the fuselage of the lead aircraft. Once the signal had been received, the latter were capable of guiding the other aircraft to their targets. This ingenious system also enabled the transmission of short Morse code messages. Pathfinders were equipped with 14 Holophane (Aldis) lamps for visual marking for landing by night, together with phosphorescent identification panels and smoke grenades for landing by day.

Groups of pathfinders from the 82nd U.S. Airborne Division's three regiments posing with the C-47 plane crews that will take them to Normandy. © NARA

THE GERMAN DEFENCE SYSTEM

The *91. LLD* continued its military training once in Cotentin. Men from the *1058. Grenadier-Regiment* taking part in manoeuvres. © Private collection

The Cotentin peninsula was defended by two German infantry divisions. The *709. Infanterie Division* (*Generalleutnant* von Schlieben) occupied the eastern coast as far as Carentan and was in charge of defending the port of Cherbourg. The *243. Infanterie Division* (*Generalleutnant* Hellmich) was in turn stationed in the Valognes sector. According to estimations by the American high command, these two divisions offered relatively mediocre combat value, for they were essentially horse-drawn and their firing power was inadequate. Their troops were essentially older or convalescent men, or very young recruits. Furthermore, the regiment had been deprived of one of its battalions, which had been replaced by battalions of Eastern volunteers (*Osttruppen*). Given their numbers and their firing power, these two divisions were entrusted with the mission of defenidng the coast, leading occasional counter-attacks, pending the arrival of reinforcements.

Yet, the German high command was perfectly aware of the strategic importance of Cherbourg, *Feldmarschall* Rommel in particular, hence his efforts to reinforce the German defence system. The 243. ID was supported by a heavy machine gun battalion and a rocket launcher regiment stationed in the sector. It was offered further cover from the 206th Armoured Division, an instruction unit the majority of whose spoiled French tanks were retroceded to the 21. *Panzerdivision* in May. The *Schnelle Brigade 30* (*Oberstleutnant* Freiherr von und zu Aufseß), positioned in the region of Coutances, was a reserve force for the *LXXXIV. Armeekorps*. Rommel had succeeded in having several units transferred to the region, including a number of engineer fortress companies, one *Nebelwerfer* (rocket launcher) regiment and two coastal artillery regiments. Several *Luftwaffe* heavy Flak batteries had also been speedily established in the Cotentin peninsula. The *Sturm Battalion AOK7* (*Major* Messerschmidt) had in turn been positioned in Cherbourg with a little over 1,100 men.

The *91. Luftlande Division* (*Generalleutnant* Falley) was deployed in the centre of the peninsula, in the region around Saint-Sauveur-le-Vicomte and Valognes late April. The division that was specialised in fighting against parachutists only boasted two grenadier regiments; however the *FallschirmjägerRegiment 6* (*Major* Von der Heydte) and the *Panzer-Ersatz-und Ausbildungs-Abteilung 100* (*Major* Bardenschlager) had been temporarily integrated, equipped with thirty French tanks.

Camouflaged M40 helmet found in Sainte-Mère-Église.
© Airborne Museum

A PARTITIONED AND FLOODED BATTLEFIELD

The village of Sainte-Mère-Église in June 1944. © NARA

The configuration of the area inland from Utah Beach is hardly propitious to an airborne attack. To the south of Valognes, the coast comprises a low plain through which the River Douve and its affluent, the Merderet, meander. The beds of both waterways are the site of vast marshlands which are, in turn, crossed by a number of drainage canals. What's more, in 1944, the Germans had deliberately flooded the lowlands off the coast, together with the beds of the Rivers Merderet and Douve.

The meadows and pastures were submerged in water and were extremely dangerous zones for the parachutists. Hundreds of two to three metre-long wooden stakes had been planted by the Germans in any clear fields likely to be used as landing grounds for gliders.

Furthermore, the landscape was covered with thick hedgerows. The small and irregular plots of land were enclosed by high earthen embankments bordered with deep ditches and surmounted with thick hedges. The intricate lacework of narrow hollow paths, together with this dense foliage rendered finding one's way impossible, by day or by night, for anyone unfamiliar with the area.

The German command took full advantage of these natural obstacles to partition the future battlefield and to concentrate the bulk of its forces in a few nerve centres. The star-shaped road network facilitated the rapid supply of reinforcements.

Consequently, the choice of drop zone and landing zones needed to take full account of the presence of enemy forces, the nature of the terrain, its natural obstacles (embankments, woods, stone walls) and the installation of Rommel's famous 'asparagus'. Near road networks and their distance from key targets were points of major importance.

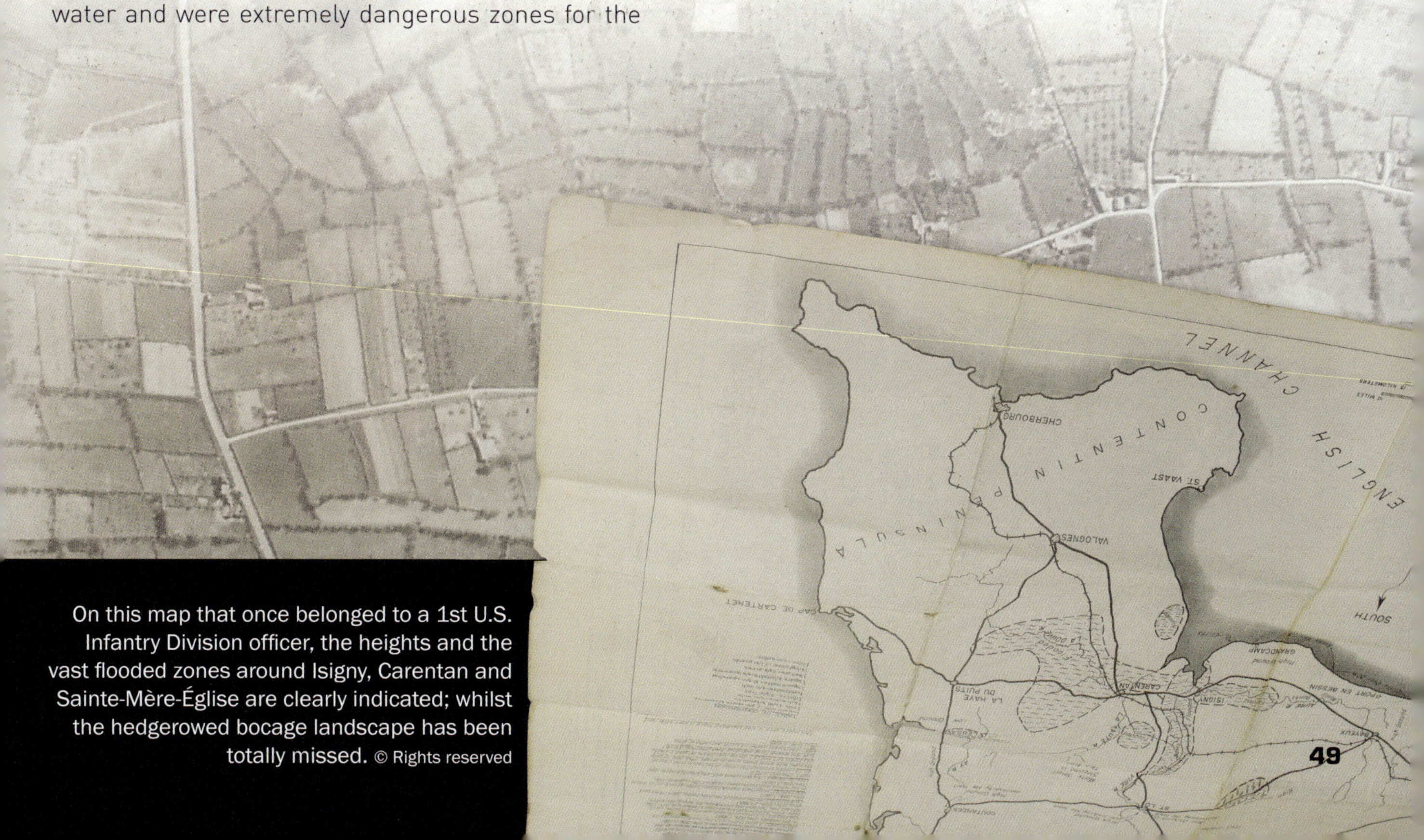

On this map that once belonged to a 1st U.S. Infantry Division officer, the heights and the vast flooded zones around Isigny, Carentan and Sainte-Mère-Église are clearly indicated; whilst the hedgerowed bocage landscape has been totally missed. © Rights reserved

SITTING PUT IN HANGARS

Mid-May, the men from the 82nd Airborne Division received orders to gather together their combat equipment. They boarded the coaches and trucks that had come to collect them. The troopers were taken to the RAF airfields in North Witham, Cottesmore, Grantham, Spanhoe, Saltby, Folkingham, Barkston Heath, Membury and Fulbeck, whilst the glidermen headed for Greenham Common, Membury, Upottery, Aldermaston, Ramsbury and Merryfield, where they found their gliders and tow planes.

Upon their arrival, the men were grouped together by company and escorted by the military police towards hangars, where hundreds of camp beds had been set up. And they were sworn to secrecy. Failing special permission, outings were prohibited. They were briefed on the rules of good conduct they were to abide by inside the base. The mess was located inside huge tents. The paras received their standard combat ration issue and new equipment such as assault gas masks, Gammon grenades and Hawkins mines. The days went by, each one

Two lieutenants (recognisable thanks to their police caps) inspecting the ammunition and material to be stored in the A-5 containers. © NARA

June 1944. A hundred Airspeed Horsa and Waco CG-4 gliders perfectly lined up and waiting in an RAF airfield. Although all planes bear the American roundel, some have not yet been painted with their invasion stripes. © NARA

seeming like the one before. Thankfully, the weather was fair. Physical exercise and sports events kept their minds and bodies at work and in good shape. Poker games met with particular success inside the hangars. The officers did their best to keep troop spirits and morale at their best. Colonel Millet from the 507th PIR had his paras' trench knives sharpened by a Notthingham-based company.

The U.S. paras used British-made leg bags like this one. © Airborne Museum

In an aviation hangar, officers from the 82nd U.S. Airborne (a Lieutenant Colonel, a Captain and a Colonel in the foreground), reunited for an ultimate brief. © NARA

For training, we used so-called sand tables. Air Corps reconnaissance and intelligence specialists carefully reviewed aerial photos and mapped out the target area where we were to jump on D-Day. The DZ was then reconstructed in miniature in a sand table for everyone to study. When we had become familiar with the details we could then become quickly oriented as soon as we had landed, even in darkness. The mock-ups were very detailed, showing streams, railroads, towns, and main highways. We worked on them for an hour and a half every day.

Private Duaine J. Pinkston, Medical Det, 1/505 PIR

On the 1st of June, large scale models depicting the towns, bridges and waterways, together with countless fields surrounded by hedges, all within an unknown destination, were installed inside the hangars. Officers and instructors explained the missions the men were to accomplish in a few days.

They were told that Normandy was their next destination. They all fully grasped that, this time, it was to be no party. They would need to fight, to capture bridges, villages, to establish barrages and to hold out for at least 12 hours without reinforcements, pending the arrival of the troops landed on the beaches. Over the days, the pressure increased through promiscuity, the interminable wait and the ever-increasing anguish that gradually seized these men, most of whom were barely twenty. Fights broke out in the hangars and the surrounding areas.

Physical activities such as baseball enabled the men to alleviate their stress levels. © Private collection

5th June, two All Americans helping each other to attach their T-5 parachute harnesses. © NARA

EMBARKATION

The announcement of the operation's postponement came as a nasty surprise. Thankfully, it would only last 24 hours. The following night, Eisenhower decided to give the go ahead. Late afternoon on the 5th of June, after a last religious service and after listening to their officers' encouragements, the para companies set to work and joined the columns of C-47s lined along the runway. A total of 379 aircraft took part in operation Boston. Similarly, the first gliders were preparing to enter the fray.

They all bore large black and white stripes on their fuselage and wings. Referred to as invasion stripes, these identification marks had been hastily painted on the Allied planes taking part in operation Neptune in order to identify them at first sight, hence avoiding friendly gunfire, as had been the case 11 months previously in Sicily. Any plane without these stripes could be shot down by the anti-aircraft defence and by fighter-bombers. Mechanics and crews were busy with the ultimate preparations, as the paras geared up and headed for the planes, where they nervously waited pending orders to board. The previous day, when everything was ready, the announcement of the operation's postponement had come as a shock. But this time, the weather was on their side.

With their blackened faces, the men, laden with the weight of their packs advanced at a cumbersome pace. They offered each other mutual assistance in boarding their craft and settled on the narrow benches on either side of the fuselage. The crews offered them a helping hand. The rear doors had been removed and the hinges covered to avoid the parachutes becoming attached when the time came to jump.

A-5 containers being filled in an airfield. © NARA

Glidermen from the 325th GIR on their way to board their gliders. © Rights reserved

In all the airfields where the troops were stationed, the same scenes repeated themselves after dusk, in perfect timing. This picture shows a training jump without weapons, for no other picture was taken of the 82nd Airborne on the evening of the 5th of June. © NARA

Evening chow was a very quiet time as I recall, with all of us thinking about what lay ahead. We knew the risks. We had been told way back through jump school at Fort Benning that very few of us would survive in combat, or if we did, it would be in an incapacitated status. Our chances of returning were dim, but no one believed that applied to him. We had heard all these stories many times in training, but it was that very training that gave us the proper mental and physical state of readiness. We were at high pitch. Our physical fitness couldn't have been better. We were in essence, ready! In fact we had spent just enough time at the airport to be in the right frame of mind to take on anybody. Let's get out of here and get on with it!

Private Leslie Palmer Cruise Jr, H Company, 3/505 PIR

US M1A1 folding stock carbine with its transport case. © Airborne Museum

THE TROOPERS AND THE GLIDERS ON D-DAY

The parachutist's standard issue pack had been enhanced. Over and above the T-5 chest parachute, they were provided with M-1936 musette bags and General Purpose bags. They also wore orange Mae West B-4 life jackets above their parachute harnesses. Since their uniforms could not house all their material, certain paras were given large canvas bags. These leg bags packed with special gear weighed in at 40 to 50 kilogrammes and were attached to one leg. During the jump, the bag was released then, held by halyards, dropped below the para, reaching the ground first and hence avoiding any unnecessary injury to the leg.

Their uniforms were impregnated with an anti-vesicant agent, were reinforced at the knees and the elbows and the cargo pockets on their trousers had been enlarged for the occasion to offer increased storage capacity. Their pockets and musette bags were packed to the gills with boxes of K rations, a change of clothing, toiletries, cigarettes and chewing gum.

Over and above the standard gas masks, flasks and portable tools, the men took with them a rope, offensive and defensive grenades, smoke bombs, extra cartridges and pouches of ammunition of all sorts. Some were issued with Colt 1911 pistols. Rifles and submachine guns were stored in carefully attached protective cases. Trench knives and Hawkins mines were most often attached by straps to the ankles. Bazooka servers were unquestionably the less fortunate for they had to jump with their cumbersome weapons. Sturdy canvas containers filled with 60mm mortars, .30 calibre machine guns, radios and ammunition were attached under the fuselage of certain aircraft, whilst others were boarded alongside the parachutists.

Their buddies in the gliders wore the standard GI's uniform, in other words the M-1941 blouson and wool serge trousers. Some glidermen were issued with the HBT uniform, also impregnated with an antigas agent. Instead of the paras' jump boots, they wore laced boots and gaiters.

RIGGERS

Each parachute unit also comprised men who were trained in the repair and maintenance of parachutes and jumping equipment. Their skills were deployed to produce or to alter existing resources. Hence, they made extra ammunition pouches and reinforced their buddies' jump uniforms by sewing sturdy canvas patches onto the elbows, knees and pockets. Introduced in Sicily during operation Husky, led by the paras from the 82nd U.S. Airborne Division, these interventions were continued in preparation of the Normandy Landings by their colleagues from the 101st U.S. Airborne Division. It is estimated that 80 to 85% of engaged troops wore reinforced uniforms on the 6th of June 1944.

Reinforced M-42 jacket. © Airborne Museum

Over and above his parachute, the trooper had to carry a whole range of other equipment. The protective case for the US M1A1 carbine, worn at the hip, suggests that this is an officer or NCO's gear. © Airborne Museum

His insignia (nationality flag and division badge) are the only ways to distinguish this BAR (Browning Automatic Rifle) gunner from the 325th GIR from a U.S. Army infantryman. © Airborne Museum

MARKING OUT DZS AND LZS

Nine C-47 Skytrains took off in groups of three from the North Witham airfield between 11.25pm and 00.07am (British time) with the pathfinders from the 82nd Airborne Division on board. Those of the 101st Airborne Division preceded them by around 30 minutes. The dull drumming sound of their Pratt & Whitney engines inundated the sleepy English countryside. The planes were headed south-west. The vanguard flight met with no resistance. The pathfinders from the 505th PIR (DZ O) landed to the north-west of Sainte-Mère-Église at 1.21am. Those from the 508th and 507th PIRs respectively arrived at 1.38am and 2.02am to mark out DZ N (Picauville) and DZ T (Amfreville).

The teams were afforded around thirty minutes to install their Eureka transponders and to set up the Holophane lamps in the form of the letter 'T', visible from the sky above. The letter's stem indicated the jump direction, whilst the horizontal bar indicated the jump limit. The Holophane lamp placed at the base of the T flashed in optical Morse code to indicate the drop zone letter. The lamps were of different colours depending on the DZ.

Commanded by First Lieutenant Smith, the pathfinders from the 505th PIR, who had been dropped 350 metres from their targets, successfully accomplished their missions on DZ O. One bright green 'T' could not be lit; however, the Eureka transponders operated every 15 minutes prior to the arrival of the regiment.

The planes transporting the pathfinders benefited from an element of surprise. However, the formations that followed them had no such advantage. © NARA

The two other drop zones were only partially equipped. First Lieutenant Joseph's pathfinders from the 507th PIR had made an accurate landing on DZ T, but the presence of many German troops nearby prevented them from using their Holophane lamps. The operators of the Eureka transponders were more fortunate. The same applied in Picauville, where the men from the 508th PIR could only light up two out of seven lamps and the major hiccup being that the marked DZ was in fact 2,500 metres from the planned zone.

Eureka-Beacon AN/PPN-1A with its battery and antenna. This compact, modular equipment was also very quick to set up. © Airborne Museum

The rear doors of the craft had been removed for air drops. The edges of all exit points were covered with thick layers of adhesive to avoid the parachute static lines from being damaged.
© NARA

CROSSING THE CHANNEL

The 369 craft transporting 6,420 paras from the 82nd Airborne followed their scouts at half-hour intervals (mission Boston). Planes took off at 10-second intervals.

The craft flew over the English Channel in arrow formation in series of nine planes, flying at an altitude of 500 feet, all lights out. For further safety, their route was marked out by radio and light beacons and a submarine.

On board, all was quiet. No one spoke, no one joked. With visibly tense expressions, the men concentrated on their ultimate instructions before boarding and repeating, mentally, each movement, each gesture adopted during training. The once loud and troublesome American paras, dreaded by the MPs (Military Police) and owners of English pubs, had somewhat lost their banter. Some dozed off, whilst others prayed in silence for their saviour. From time to time, they exchanged a few words to lighten the atmosphere, striving not to show the fear that engulfed them all. As they looked out the portholes, the men could see the flash of the formation lights at the tip of the C-47 wings. Beneath them, they imagined more than they could actually distinguish the hundreds of ships sailing towards Normandy.

When they came within reach of the Channel Islands, the pilots changed course north-west of Guernsey (operation Hoboken) in order to approach the Cotentin peninsula from the south-west, as they increased their altitude to 1,500 feet. Strong gusts of wind forced them to clutch onto their controls, continuously correcting their planes' trajectories and attitudes.

All the paras were issued with a silk Zones of France escape map at a scale of 1/2,000,000. It could be hidden inside a garment's lining.
© Private collection

GO, GO, GO!

The C-47 Skytrains passed over the Channel Islands and their formidable Flak batteries, without the slightest incident. As they approached the coast, the planes entered a zone of heavy fog, which resulted in dislocating their formations. The anti-aircraft defence batteries in Cotentin entered into action. The skies were illuminated with the explosion of shells and tracer bullets. The projector beams swept across the dark of night in search of these unwelcome birds. Several aircraft flying at low altitude were victims to direct hits, only to plunge, ablaze, into water or land.

In those flying at around 250km/h, the control lights changed from red to green. Jumpmasters ordered for the men to stand up. Shaken from left to right, the paras struggled to stay upright, attached their static lines to the central metal cable located on the roof of the plane and made one last check of their equipment as they waited for the crucial instant to come. When the light turned green, the men thrust forth like robots, jumping into the void one after another, through the lateral door.

Hesitation was simply not an option. Hence, they plunged earthwards, soon to find themselves suspended beneath their canopies amidst a sky illuminated with tracer bullets and Flak shells exploding all around. The inexperienced pilots attempted somewhat precarious evasive manoeuvres, distancing themselves from the drop zones. However, they were forbidden from returning to England with their sticks. Their twin-engined planes bore the brunt of enemy anti-aircraft defence fire, some turning into balls of fire. The most experienced among them did their utmost to take the men to their targets, at any cost.

Shortly after 2 in the morning, First Lieutenant Robert Mathias from the 508th PIR's E Company was hit when preparing to jump from his aircraft. His blood-covered body was found later on the ground, still attached to his parachute. After dropping his stick of paras from the same regiment, Lieutenant W. Dunagan from the 50th Troop Carrier Squadron (314th TCG) attempted a second round to drop two remaining paras. He was killed outright by a stray bullet in his cockpit. His copilot took the plane back to base. Dunagan was awarded the Distinguished Service Cross for this heroic act. A total of eight craft were destroyed and fifteen damaged.

Garand M1 rifles were stored dissassembled in quilted Griswold pouches like this one. © Airborne Museum

THE POCKET KNIFE M2

The paras needed knives to cut their parachute straps when required to rapidly free themselves from the canopy. The U.S. Army placed an order with Geo Schrade Co. for the production of a switchblade pocket knife. Approved in December 1940, it was officially named the Pocket Knife M2. After landing in water, PVT Thomas Porcella from the 508th PIR's Company H narrowly escaped drowning by successfully cutting the thick straps of his harness with his M2 knife.

M2 switchblade jump knife made by Schrade Walden in New York. © Airborne Museum

Paras watching what is going on outside from the portholes. The relative lack of material confirms that this picture was taken during training. © NARA

The drop was doomed to be a disaster when the C-47 pilot began to take evasive action to avoid the heavy Flak. He gave us the green light when the plane was in a climbing attitude as the engines roared at top speed. When I jumped, the prop blast was so severe that it tore off my pack and equipment so that when I hit the ground, the only weapon I had was my jump knife. I didn't see any other member of my stick.

Lieutenant Edward V. Ott, HQ Company, 2/508 PIR

Chest parachute made by the Pioneer Parachute Co.
© Airborne Museum

LOST IN THE DARK OF NIGHT

Dropped to the north of Sainte-Mère, Sergeant Robert D. Henderson and PFC Harvill W. Lazenby from the 1/505 PIR were captured on the 6th of June. They escaped from a column of prisoners on the night of the 11th to the 12th of June, but it took them 37 hours to get back to their own lines. © NARA

At about 0315 hours, June 6, 1944, it seemed pitch black – I had never seen anything like the huge mounds of hedgerows before; they were mounds of earth with thickets running from bottom to top in a 'jungle' of bushes, thorns and even trees, they were bigger and meaner than those we had known in England, and they would cause much trouble, blocking direct passage from any one point to another, even making passage for tanks difficult!

Sergeant William H. Tucker, 505th PIR

The 505th PIR's drop was a fine example of accuracy and success. The planes had flown above the fields, hence escaping anti-aircraft fire. Eighty out of 120 sticks were dropped on, or within 2 kilometres, of a perfectly marked-out DZ O. The two other regiments were less fortunate, due to disastrous drops.

Most of the C-47s that were transporting the 507th PIR missed DZ T, due to gunfire from the Flak, causing their formations to divide. One battalion had been dropped well out of its zone, due to the excessive speed of its planes. Around fifty C-47s nevertheless managed to release their stick within the correct drop zone. Lieutenant Colonel Arthur A. Maloney, in command of the 3/507 PIR, successfully rallied together a few men in the La Fière sector, whilst the bulk of his unit, comprising a total of 160 men, had been mistakenly dropped around Graignes, 7km to the south of Carentan.

The 508th PIR planes were also a prime target for the Flak above Saint-Sauveur-le-Vicomte. Only forty planes effectively reached their drop zone. A quarter of the regiment landed 1.5km from DZ N, whilst another quarter was almost 3km away. Some even landed 15km off course.

As I started making my way through the field I ran into a squad of Germans. I attempted to shoot at the first one I saw, but suddenly, I felt a searing pain in my leg. The next thing I knew I was surrounded by Germans pointing rifles at my head. I thought this was the end. The German soldiers took my watch and billfold, yelled at me and asked if I was American. I tried to stand up but my leg would not support my weight. My captors found a stick and tied it to my leg and carried me across the field. War was a strange thing. We were supposed to kill each other, but now these enemy solider were looking after me.

PFC Clarence S. Hughart, 507th PIR

Half of the regiment found itself to the east of the River Merderet, incapable of accomplishing its assigned mission. Colonel Roy Lindquist was deprived of a vast share of his officers. Lieutenant Colonel Herbert Batcheller, commander of the 1/508 PIR was killed next to his radio operator by an embankment. Lieutenant Colonel Louis Mendez from the 3/508 PIR landed safe and sound to the north of the River Douve, despite the three projectiles that had transperced his musette bag. He strayed for five days without coming across a single member of his battalion. A share of Company G had been dropped above the English Channel and one stick had landed, spot on, in the midst of the *91. LLD* staff headquarters in Picauville.

Losses sustained during airdrops were of 272 men, i.e. 4.24% of the total force. The paras lost around 60% of their material in the marshy zones. Despite the glow of the moon, the coloured canopies of the containers scattered across the countryside and flooded zones were impossible to distinguish from those of the parachutes that had been abandoned

The rising tide has washed the body of this parachutist - still attached to his harness - up on the pebbled beach. A total of forty of the men from the 82nd U.S. Airborne Divsion drowned. © NARA

all around. Some paras landed in flooded zones; others found themselves suspended from the branches of trees, or on rooftops. Others landed several dozen kilometres from their drop zones. For some, this delve into the void ended in more or less serious fractures or commotion.

Torches were fixed onto the containers. Their colours, and those of the canopies, indicated the container's contents.
© Private collection

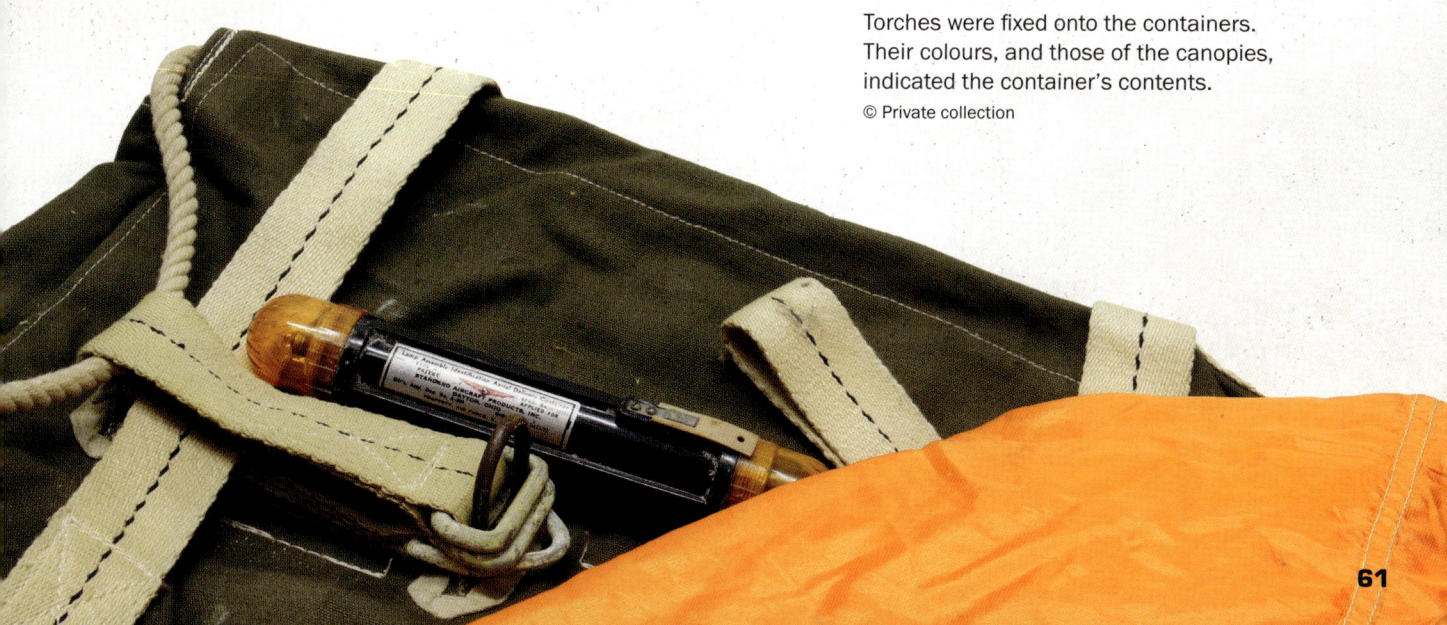

THE HÉMEVEZ MASSACRE

One stick from the 1/507 PIR landed by the hamlet of Le Ham. Three paras by the names of Landry, Wright and Moore found themselves near the village of Hémevez when they saw seven of their fellow soldiers executed by the Germans. Their bodies fell into a ditch, dug out for the occasion. After the Germans left, the locals exhumed their bodies to have them buried in the church graveyard. An inquiry was made by the U.S. Army. Major Felix, the German officer in charge of the sector, was identified and found in a camp in Canada. However, whether he was executed before his trial or died before answering for his deeds, remains a mystery.

Lieutenant Colonel Benjamin H. 'Vandy' Vandervoort, in command of the 2/505 PIR, fractured his left ankle upon landing. The least fortunate were killed before even setting foot on French soil, or drowned, unable to free themselves from their parachutes.

Lost in the dark, isolated paras hid in ditches and bushes to escape enemy patrols pending the junction with their fellow troops. The sound of gunfire echoed through the night. Men fell, knifed or shot down at point blank range. Over the early hours of the invasion, the paras had received orders not to burden themselves with prisoners or with wounded enemy troops. In turn, certain German soldiers did not hesitate to execute or even mutilate captured parachutists.

Amidst all this confusion, officers reunited the men they recovered along their way. Groups ranging from the size of a section to 100 men, from varying original units, silently marched through the maze of hedgerows and flooded ground. In command of a group of 150 men,

Each man was issued with a USAAF Model 2 bandage pack. It contained a small bandage, a tourniquet and a small syrette of morphine.
© Airborne Museum

When I landed, nobody was around. It is amazing how you can be spread out from your fellow jumpers. I felt very tired and just lay still for a few seconds before getting out of my chute. I got orientated and crawled over to the edge of a pasture. The moon was out, I distinguished a gate and there sat a machine gun - it was one of ours. Soon I heard somebody coming my way and I said, 'Flash'. A voice said, 'Don't shoot, please don't shoot! I forgot the damn countersign.' It was Bob Lehman (Robert F. Lehman), another member from my stick We could hear some shooting in the distance but saw nobody around. Once in a while one of our planes got hit, knocked out by enemy Flak.'

Private Duaine J. Pinkston, Medical Det, 1/505 PIR

Brigadier General Gavin progressed southwards along the railway track towards La Fière, which was in the hands of a 505th PIR company.

The Germans began to hear the noise of the formidable armada of Allied planes flying overhead. In Picauville, several parachutists landed in the middle of the staff of the German *91.LLD*. The alert was raised. The Germans scrutinised the dozens of parachute canopies as they dropped to the ground. The German troops challenged their adversaries wherever they found them. The dispersal of enemy units was a serious hindrance to engaging reserve troops to challenge them. The *91. LLD* and the *709. ID* were ordered to counter-attack, yet no concerted action was possible until they had a clear picture of the Allied forces they were facing, and of their targets. At 1.30am, the presence of parachute drops in Cotentin was reported to the *7. Armee* headquarters. Although the Americans were clearly seeking to isolate the peninsula at its narrowest point, it was impossible to determine the centre of gravity and the orientation of its offensive.

Occasionally one large flash appeared and I would see a plane sihouetting earthward. 'Oh my God,' I thought, 'there goes a whole plane load of guys.' I was rudely brought back to the happenings around me as one by one troops came down crashing into hedgerows or banging into the ground unceremonioulsy, cursing as they floated in. As far as I could discern in the darkness, I was situated in what appeared to be a three-acre field. To my right was the twenty foot hedgerow I had so recently missed. To my rear was some kind of road which was some six foot below the field. I could see the shadows of several men as they emerged from the hedgerows about the field heading towards me and then I recalled that I was in the middle of the stick of parachutists and they would gravitate in my direction. This was standard procedure to gather in the middle man. I gave the cricket snap and heard the reply in two clicks. One gave the sign 'Flash' and I replied 'Thunder', sign and counter sign given as the troops assembled in my area by ones, twos and larger groups. Within a short time our platoon was intact along with many from other third battalion companies.

Private Leslie Palmer Cruise Jr., H Company, 505th PIR

FIRST ENCOUNTERS

The study of scale models and maps was of little use on the terrain. Lost in the dark, deprived of any visual landmark, the parachutists could only rely on their compasses and their instinct. Constantly on the alert, they worked their way along the hedges, knocking at farm doors for information. The inhabitants, who had been wakened by the buzz of the planes and the tumult of armed combat, anxiously awaited for events to unfold, or took refuge in trenches hollowed out in their gardens. There was no longer any doubt that the long-awaited Allied landings had begun. By means of airdropped leaflets, the Allied high command had enlightened the French on the arrival of parachutists, describing them as the vanguard of their Liberation.

Paras from the 82nd Airborne Division asking a Norman civilian for information. © NARA

This Horsa glider, carrying glider troops from the 325th GIR's A Company, has turned over after hitting large trees, killing eight of its occupants. © NARA

CHAPTER 4

THE BATTLE OF SAINTE-MÈRE-ÉGLISE

THE FIRST SKIRMISHES

Since the middle of the night, the Sainte-Mère fire brigade, equipped with a hand pump, had been struggling to contain the fire that was raging in Julia Pommier's house and a nearby barn. As soon as the alarm had been sounded, the two leading local resistance fighters, Maury and Deloeuvre, together with many villagers and the mayor, Alexandre Renaud, had all flocked to help the firemen. They formed a human chain and passed buckets of water from the cattle market pump to the fire, under surveillance from the German soldiers.

At 1.20am, the sound of a plane formation could be heard coming from the west. The buzz of the plane engines intensified to become deafening. The local inhabitants were soon to see the massive outline of twin-engined planes flying at low altitude.

Six planes from the 439th TCG, transporting men from the 2/506 PIR's F Company (mission Albany), mistakenly dropped sticks 74 and 75 above the village. The puffed green and white canopies appeared in their wake, slowly descending towards the ground. The Germans on site opened fire, whilst the frightened civilians ran to shelter.

Once on the ground, the paras from the 101st Airborne realised that they had been dropped in the wrong place, instead of in DZ C by Hiesville. They were immediately challenged by the enemy. PFCs Hale, Buchter and Kermode, and PVT–Hult were killed. Raymond R Aebischer managed to escape safe and sound. At the south village entrance, a C-47, hit by the Flak, crashed into a field, ablaze. Its pilot, Second Lieutenant Marvin F. Muir, his five crew members and a parachutist who had failed to jump in time, all died in the crash.

Thirty minutes later, at 1.51am, a new plane formation from the 316th TCG (mission Boston), carrying paras from the 2/505 PIR, flew over the village. The C-47, flown by First Lieutenant Calvin S. Heinlein, dropped a stick of 16 parachutists from F Company.

The paras fell all around, in the surrounding gardens and streets. Dr Monnier, the village vet, was with his wife and daughter in a trench

This T-5 parachute was found in the centre of Sainte-Mère-Église immediately after the fighting. The stencilled letters 'RS' indicate that this para belonged to the 506th PIR, commanded by Colonel Robert Sink. © Airborne Museum

hollowed out at the foot of their garden when PFC Clifford A. Maughan landed a few metres away. *Leutnant* Werner, who was accommodated there, bolted forward, pistol in hand, and surprised the parachutist as he struggled to untangle himself. The vet stepped in and cried, 'Don't fire! Don't fire!' As the two soldiers faced each other, the tension was tangible. The vet's daughter, who spoke English, served as an interpreter. After a brief exchange, the American explained that a substantial airborne force had been dropped in the sector and that it was no exercise. After a few moment's thought, the German officer grasped the imminent danger, returned his gun and surrendered.

The officer in command of the stick, Second Lieutenant Harold O. Cadish, together with PVTs Ladislaw Tlapa, Harvey T. Bryant, Charles P. Blankenship and Penrose D. Shearer, were shot down at point blank range, still hanging from the trees and electric poles around the village square. PFC Alfred J. Van Holsbeck landed amidst the blazing house. Stuck in a tree, PVT Ernest R. Blanchard cut off his finger as he was struggling to free himself from his parachute harness.

Sainte-Mère-Église fireman's helmet.
© Airborne Museum

The 93rd TCS C-47 (42-100876) flown by Second Lieutenant Marvin F. Muir, crashed at 1.12am at the entrance to the village on the Caen road, after dropping its 2/506PIR stick. © NARA

In the Normandy bocage, danger was all around and the enemy could be lurking behind any one of the many hedges. These paras were killed simultaneously. © NARA

I was a bazooka gunner for the second platoon, Company F of the 505th PIR of the 82nd Airborne Division. For the jump, I was the 5th or 6th guy just after Lieutenant Harold Cadish, our jumpmaster. We were dropped over Sainte-Mère-Église, a house fire lit up the square. I landed on the roof of the church, and I was hanging by my parachute. While I was trying to reach my knife to get rid of my straps, another paratrooper hit the steeple and also remained suspended, not far from me. His canopy was hanging from a gargoyle of the steeple, it was my friend John Steele.

PVT Kenneth E. Russell, F Company, 505th PIR

Wounded by shrapnel during his fall, PFC John M. Steele, remained suspended by his parachute on the church steeple, in a state of semi-consciousness. Meanwhile, his buddy, PVT Kenneth E. Russell, also landed on the roof of the church, above the main doorway. At that same instant, Sergeant John P. Ray set foot on the centre of the village square just a few metres from a German soldier. As he struggled as best he could to free himself from his harnass, Ray grabbed his Colt 45 pistol and fired at the German as the latter aimed direct at Russell. Russell managed to escape and Ray, seriously wounded, collapsed. Initially left for dead, Ray was finally evacuated a few hours later; however, he died from his wounds on the 13th of June.

This military ID plate (dog tag) belonged to John Steele. Wounded in the foot, he was taken prisoner. He escaped three days later and managed to join the Allied lines.
© Airborne Museum

The rest of the stick, i.e. T/4 Edward J. White, Corporal Vernon L. Francisco and PVTs Philip M. Lynch, Steven Epps and Daryle E. Whitfield landed safe and sound between the church and the graveyard. The soldiers from the *30. Flak Regiment* took advantage of a lull to head to their trucks and flee Sainte-Mère-Église. *Gefreiter* Rudolf May and the young Heinz Strangfeld, both posted in the church steeple, withdrew to their command post in Fauville, accompanied by *Unteroffizier* Rudi Escher.

The 4th U.S. Infantry Division joined the paras at Sainte-Mère on the 7th of June. GIs re-enacting the capture of the village for War Photographers.
© NARA

THE 508TH IN COMBAT

Rommel left the Château de Bernaville on the 17th of May 1944. Falley is standing behind him to his right. © Bundesarchiv

At around midnight, *Generalleutnant* Wilhelm Falley left the Château de Bernaville, where he had set up his command post, to attend a *Kriegspiel* in Rennes. He was accompanied by his chauffeur, *Gefreiter* Vogt, and his aide de camp, *Oberleutnant* Joachim Bartuzat. After a 2-hour drive, their Horch made a u-turn, probably by Avranches. Could they have noticed the planes, or heard the sound of the battle, or even been informed of the situation during a stopover? No one knows. Falley was to reach his mobile command post, concealed in a hollow path not far from the castle.

At around 2.30am, First Lieutenant Malcolm Dodge Brannen, commander of the HQ Company, 3/508 PIR, landed in an apple tree. After managing to free himself, the officer wandered through the countryside, finding 11 paras from the 508th PIR and the 307th Engineer Battalion along his way. This small group of astray soldiers eventually stumbled upon a mill to the north of Picauville. After engaging in a short conversation with the Lagouche family, they heard the sound of an engine. The paras immediately took up position to intercept the vehicle.

With his Thompson in hand, Brannen came out of his shelter and ordered for the driver to stop; however, the latter accelerated. The paras all fired together on the Horch which crashed into the building wall. Bartuzat, the front passenger was killed outright. Unscathed, Vogt was captured in the cellar where he was trying to hide. Wounded, Falley lay in the middle of the road. He yelled to the Americans not to kill him as he crawled along the ground towards his Luger pistol. Brannen ordered for the German officer to halt. As his hand reached out towards his gun, the American shot him in the head, killing him. He was unaware that he had just deprived the *91. LLD* of its commander. He only discovered his victim's identity by inspecting his helmet.

The dispersal of the 508th PIR was such that it could no longer accomplish its mission to destroy the two bridges over the River Douve at Pont-l'Abbé

THE FIELD RATION D BAR

This was an emergency ration devised by Colonel Paul Logan from the Quartermaster Corps and the Hershey Chocolate Corporation. This chocolate bar weighing around four ounces was extremely dense and offered an energy value equivalent to 600 calories. It could also withstand high temperatures. Its taste was barely more pleasant than that of a boiled potato to avoid men from eating it too easily. Its composition was as follows: oat flour, liqueur and cocoa butter, powdered skimmed milk, sugar and artificial flavouring. The bar was issued in paraffin-coated cardboard packaging that was sufficiently compact for soldiers to store it in one of their pockets.

The instruction insert in the Field Ration D specified that it was to be eaten very slowly (15 minutes). If necessary, it could be dissolved in hot water. © Private collection

THE FIRST SPOILS OF WAR

As his buddies gathered all the documents they found inside the vehicle, Private Jack W. Schlegel took a flag and hid it on the spot of the accident. A few days later, he was captured by the Germans and the convoy was attacked by Allied fighter-bombers. After three failed attempts, he finally managed to escape with help from a German doctor from a hospital in Rennes. He then set off in search of Patton's troops. On his way back through the Cotentin peninsula to board for England, he returned to the mill to fetch his war spoils, which he donated to the Airborne Museum in Sainte-Mère-Église in 1969.

and Beuzeville-la-Bastille. The men would need to improvise. Lieutenant Colonel Shanley, commander of the 2/508th PIR, who had landed to the east of Picauville, was marching towards Pont-l'Abbé, in head of a troop comprised of 300 men. The column was stopped in its tracks by an imposing German force of the size of a battalion. Shanley therefore decided to walk eastwards and to find a way to cross the Merderet. Mid afternoon, the small paratroop force, which had been joined by Major Shields Warren's group, set up position on Hill 30, a height located by the hamlet of Caponnet on the west bank of the river. This isolated promontory in the middle of the marshes stands to the north of the causeway leading to Chef-du-Pont, in the immediate vicinity of the *91. LLD* command post. The Germans attacked the positions held by the paras, but failed to dislodge them. A support column sent by Colonel Roy E. Lindquist reached the opposite bank before being stopped in its tracks. The paras set up a barrage on the road but, on the 8th of June, a violent counter-attack forced them to retreat to the east bank of the Merderet. The situation had become critical. Shells hailed down on Shanley and his men, whose food and ammunition supplies were dwindling. A patrol of 23 parachutists led by First Lieutenant Woodrow W. Millsaps succeeded in securing the area on

Colonel Lindquist commanded the 508th PIR until December 1945. This highly decorated officer's career came to an end at the rank of Major General. © NARA

either side of the road, hence enabling a convoy to bring in fresh supplies. The road was nevertheless still subjected to enemy gunfire. It was only on the 10th of June that reinforcements reached Shanley's group and permanently drove the German troops out of Picauville.

CAPTURING SAINTE-MÈRE-ÉGLISE

Shortly after 2 in the morning, the paras from the 505th PIR who had landed in DZ O gradually joined forces. The regiment's commander, Colonel William E. Ekman, set off towards Sainte-Mère-Église with a few men from his stick. En route, they came across Major Frederick C.A. Kellam from the 1/505 PIR, on his way to the La Fière bridge, and with Lieutenant Colonel Vandervoort, who was wounded. Since he refused to be evacuated, the officer's men had placed him on a cart in order to facilitate his transport. Their aim was to take control of the small market town of Neuville-au-Plain, located two kilometres to the north of Sainte-Mère-Église.

Lieutenant Colonel Edward C. 'Cannonball' Krause, commander of the 3/505 PIR, was also heading towards Sainte-Mère with 150 men. A local inhabitant informed him that a share of the garrison had already left. They reached the north of the village at around 4am. Krause formed six combat groups. Five of them were entrusted with establishing defensive barrages at the village entrances, whilst the sixth was to take control of the locality. Krause ordered for his men to progress silently and to use their knives whenever possible. As they advanced down the main street, they sectioned the telephone line that linked the village with Cherbourg. The paras searched the houses, taking the last remaining German soldiers by surprise. Several were taken prisoner and 11 were killed.

Despite his broken ankle, Lieutenant Colonel Vandervoort remained on the front lines. © NARA

Lieutenant Colonel Krause wearing a reinforced uniform. Note the handle of the spoon that he has placed in one of the openings on the chest pocket. © NARA

Map case made with a piece of camouflaged parachute fabric.
© Airborne Museum

At 4.30am, the Star-Spangled Banner that once flew in the city of Naples replaced the Nazi flag on the façade of the town hall. Krause immediately sent a messenger to inform Ekman of the good news, 'We're in Sainte-Mère-Église and we're holding the village.' The messenger failed to locate the commander of the 505th PIR, but did come across Major General Ridgway. Their encounter led to a series of detrimental orders and counter-orders. With no news from the rest of the unit, Vandervoort decided to head towards Sainte-Mère to capture the village. He cautiously gave orders to First Lieutenant Turner B. Turnbull from D Company to keep watch over the RN13 trunk road leading to Neuville-au-Plain. His platoon was in position shortly before 10am.

In Sainte-Mère, Krause reinforced the defensive barrages after the arrival of a number of lost paras. He positioned First Lieutenant Ivan F. Woods' G Company to the south, to cover the roads towards Carentan and Gambosville. H and HQ Companies, commanded by Captains Walter C. DeLong and Talton 'Woody' Long, held the north, east and west access routes. Captain Harold H. Swingler's I Company was placed in reserve. Vandervoort and his men arrived shortly before 8.30am. After a brief discussion, Vandy and Cannonball placed the 2/505 PIR to the north and east, whilst the 3/505 PIR was positioned to the south and west. With a few of his men, the Lieutenant Colonel recovered a jeep and two 57mm antitank guns, brought in by glider. He positioned the first gun to the north, level with the retirement home by Neuville, and the second to the south, on the Carentan road.

These gliders from the 325th GIR are wearing their Mae West life jackets. Four are smoking to keep calm. In the background, note the curtain in front of the Horsa cabin. © NARA

MISSION DETROIT

Fifty-two C-47 Skytrains from the 437th TCG towed the Waco gliders that were engaged in Mission Detroit (82nd Airborne Division) over the Cotentin peninsula. They were transporting two anti-aircraft batteries, 22 jeeps, 16 antitank guns, 220 staff members and 10 tonnes of equipment and ammunition. For the Flak, constantly on the lookout, they offered a prime target. Although they successfully hit 38 craft, only one crashed. Twenty-three Wacos landed on LZ O as from 4.07am. Seven ran off course after being released too soon, whilst seven others landed on the left bank of the River Merderet. Extensive damage was to be expected. Whilst only half of the vehicles and two antitank guns were still fit for use, human losses were relatively low; three dead and twenty-three wounded.

THE ALL AMERICANS IN SAINTE-MÈRE

Opposite: this picture, often used to illustrate the liberation of Sainte-Mère by the American paras, is in fact a picture of men from the 4th U.S. Infantry Division as they prepare to enter the Leménicier hardware store. The shop front is riddled with shrapnel. © NARA

Below: due to lack of vehicles, the All Americans used horses and German horse-drawn vehicles to transport material and the wounded. Although Sainte-Mère was in safe Allied hands, the men from the 505th PIR maintained the utmost prudence. As they advanced, they scrutinised each and every window. © NARA

Paras helping a family to return to its home. © NARA

Captain Chappie, B. Wood, the 505th PIR's Protestant chaplain (standing right) did his best to offer solace to the men and to accompany the dying. For services, he wore a robe made from pieces of fabric recovered from container parachute canopies.
© NARA

Major Daniel B. McIlvoy, a surgeon from the 505th PIR, giving a cigarette to a German officer at the hospice entrance. Captain P. Suer, the regiment's dentist, is observing the scene. © NARA

The hospice in Sainte-Mère (which today houses the town hall) was transformed into a medical outpost to care for the American and German wounded. © NARA

Soldiers from the *Luftwaffe* waiting in ambush. © Private collection

THE FIRST GERMAN COUNTER-ATTACKS

Suddenly, at around 9.30am, German shells showered down on the locality. To the south, the positions held by the 3/505 PIR were attacked by the *GR.1058 1. Bataillon* and two *Ost-Bataillon 795* companies essentially composed of Georgian volunteers, with support from three tanks and two self-propelled guns.

The paras were issued with Colt M1911A1 pistols. Their leather holsters offered them a stylishly outmoded look.
© Private collection

The antitank gun servers destroyed several armoured vehicles; however, the infantry was determined to recapture the village and continued its advance alongside the hedgerows. Although they were given a seriously hard time, the paras finally managed to stop them in their tracks, despite lesser numbers in the American ranks. PFC Dominick DiTullio from HG Company distinguished himself by leading a grenade attack. For his heroic action, he was awarded the Distinguished Service Cross, sadly posthumously, for he was killed on the 7th of June.

Eager to relieve the pressure on his men, Krause entrusted Captain Harold H. Swingler from I Company with the mission of attacking Hill 20 (Fauville) in order to put an end, once and for all, to the enemy artillery fire. But on their way, Swingler's platoon fell into an ambush. The officer was killed and the escaped paras managed to retreat with the wounded.

Major John Norton and Captains Robert 'Doc' Franco and Alexander Pete Suer taking stock of the situation. © NARA

with his Lieutenant, Vandervoort positioned his men along the hedges on either side of the road.

Shortly after his arrival, he was informed by a civilian, as he passed by on his bicycle, that a column of German prisoners led by a group of paras was approaching the position. Yet Vandervoort, very sceptical, decided to scrutinise the road with his binoculars - indeed, he could see the column around 500 metres from his position. Behind the column, he noticed the presence of tanks. It was a trick devised by the Germans to force the paras to reveal their positions. A few warning shots sufficed to unmask them. The grenadiers from the *GR.1058 3. Bataillon* retaliated before taking to the ditches for cover.

German gunfire intensified, relentlessly harassing the American positions. Heavy losses were sustained among the paras from the 82nd Airborne Division. Sergeant Stanley S. Smith, PFC William C. Walter and PVTs Robert L. Herrin and Robert E. Holtzmann from G Company were all killed next to their mortar.

Vandervoort boarded a jeep at around 1pm and headed for Neuville-au-Plain to inspect the defensive positions. His vehicle was towing a 57mm antitank gun, that was to prove a welcome initiative. Turnbull was in command of 42 men, one .30 calibre machine gun, several Browning automatic rifles, a bazooka, and a 60mm mortar. After a short brief

The Hawkins No. 75 mine was a versatile weapon. It could be thrown like a simple grenade or used as a mine or a demolition charge. It took several grenades to bring a tank to a halt.
© Airborne Museum

THE FIRST CIVILIAN DEATHS

It was business as usual for the village hardware merchant, Jules Leménicier. Opposite, the café-hairdresser M. Jamard and his family were all seated at the dining table when a salvoe of shells was sent showering across the Carentan road. A shell exploded in the middle of the road, between the hardware store and the café. Both façades were riddled with shrapnel which shattered the doors and windows. Mortally wounded, Jules Leménicier collapsed inside his store. In the café opposite, René Jamard, who was seated at the top of the table, was hit by a piece of shrapnel and died instantly. Christiane Dorey, aged 22, was killed in front of her house window. The German guns continued to fire on the village centre. M. Potigny and the Raffray couple also paid the ultimate price. Firing continued unremittingly until the following afternoon. A total of 22 of Sainte-Mère's inhabitants were killed during the early days of the Battle of Normandy.

The *Panzerjäger-Abteilung 709* Marder I tank destroyers began to fire on the American positions, killing the bazooka servers. The antitank gunners immediately struck back putting the first tank out of action.

The grenadiers launched a frontal attack, in vain. Changing tactics, they then formed several small groups, in an effort to surprise the paras side-on.

Vandervoort returned to Sainte-Mère and sent First Lieutenant Theodore L. Peterson's platoon to the rescue, via the cover of the hedges, to assist Turnbull. In Neuville, the situation rapidly turned critical. In far greater numbers, the Germans overwhelmed the paras, inflicting heavy losses, but the latter hung on. At around 4pm, Peterson and his men arrived to cover the retreating troops, Turnbull heavy-heartedly leaving behind the seriously wounded with a nurse. The able-bodied withdrew, protected by the gunfire cover provided by the rearguard troops. Technical Sergeant Robert Bob Niland was killed behind his machine gun as he covered his unit's retreat. When he returned to Sainte-Mère, only 16 men from his platoon were still fit for combat.

Turnbull, who was nicknamed 'Chief' by his men, due to his American Indian origins, was killed by a mortar shell the following morning. He was posthumously awarded the Silver Star.

Late afternoon, Krause was wounded for the third time. This time, a bullet had hit his left leg. He was evacuated and taken to the hospice, transformed into a field hospital, for the night. Major William J. Hagan temporarily took over command of the 3/505 PIR. Vandervoort asked an artillery observer liaising with the *USS Nevada* battleship located off Utah Beach to fire on Neuville-au-Plain. At 9.45pm, the first salvo of eighteen 355mm shells hit the RN13 trunk road. A few minutes later, a second salvo of shells hit the sector further north, stopping the enemy's offensive efforts for at least a few hours.

Krause proudly flaunting the third wound he suffered on the 6th of June 1944. He was awarded the Distinguished Service Cross.
© NARA

Since 11am, enemy artillery fire and gunfire from light weapons had been as continuous as accurate, rendering no Allied advance possible. At around 5pm, an attempt to bring supplies to the besieged paras in Sainte-Mère-Église was launched. [...] The very sight of the C-47s releasing their gliders was enough to divert the enemy's attention and to provoke flurries of intense gunfire in the latter's direction. Meanwhile, a messenger arrived with orders to send the 1st Platoon's mortar team to the 2nd Platoon's sector immediately east of the trunk road. The sergeant in charge of the 1st Platoon had the instructions sent to the mortar team chief, Sergeant Stanley Smith. When Smith began complaining about this new mission, the platoon chief replied, laughing, 'Don't worry! If anything happens, I promise I'll take flowers to your grave.' However, this new manoeuvre did not fail to draw the Germans' attention and, a few seconds later, a deluge of artillery fire struck the mortar team, obliging them to advance. Too late, the enemy gunfire reached unprecedented intensity. The road and nearby rooftops were the theatre of explosions of all sorts, shrapnel whirling all around. A fragment of shell went through Private Robert Herrin's trouser pocket, provoking the explosion of the Gammon grenade it contained. Herrin and Smith were killed outright. The two other team members, Walter and Holtzmann, died shortly afterwards at the first aid post. One blast sent the platoon chief hurling above the wall of a nearby property. He survived the attack with minor contusions.

Ronald C. Snyder, 505th PIR

The smoking wreck of a *Sturmgeschutz III* assault gun by the roadside on the way to Neuville-au-Plain. This armoured vehicle was destroyed during the attack by the *GR.1058*. © NARA

© Rights reserved

BENJAMIN H. VANDERVOORT (1917-1990)

This New-Yorker, who had dreamed of an artistic career, enlisted in the U.S. Army in 1937, to join the brand-new airborne force in the summer of 1940. He rapidly worked his way up the ranks to be promoted to the grade of First Lieutenant the following year, then Captain in August 1942. He took command of the 505th PIR's F Company. He integrated the staff of the 504th PRCT in April 1943 and took part in the Italian invasion. He then returned to the 2/505 PIR as its commander. Vandy was promoted to the grade of Lieutenant Colonel on the 2nd of June 1944. He particularly distinguished himself during combat in Sainte-Mère-Église, in Holland and in the Battle of the Bulge. He was awarded the Bronze Star, three Purple Hearts, two Distinguished Service Crosses (DSC) and three foreign distinctions for his bravery and the wounds he sustained. Ridgway said of Vandervoort that he was, 'one of the bravest and toughest battle commanders I ever knew.' He left the army at the end of the war to devote himself to a number of positions in foreign affairs, before working for the CIA and the Department of Defense in the 1960s. He was killed in an accident at Hilton Head in 1990. He was elevated to the rank of National Hero.

The Germans then launched a series of movements aimed at isolating, then destroying the American bridgehead by night. Von Schlieben personally coordinated this counter-attack. Early on the morning of the 7th of June, the Germans bombarded the rail bridge by General Gavin's command post.

With support from two motorised heavy artillery battalions, a company of self-propelled guns and a few *Ost-Bataillon 795* units, the *GR. 1058* launched a new attack. First Lieutenant Oliver B. Carr's paras, who were in control of the sector north-east of the town were subjected to an exemplary enemy artillery bombardment. However, their staunch resistance finally discouraged the Germans, who ended up retreating before a vain attempt to break through to the west. But after taking the time to rally round and reorganise, the enemy launched a further attack. Covered by two *Sturmgeschütz III* assault guns, the German infantry progressed through the ditches. Yet the 2/505 PIR firmly maintained its positions. One of the tanks was stopped in its tracks just 50 metres from Vandervoort's command post. Out on a reconnaissance mission, First Lieutenant Waverly Wray found himself isolated in the midst of the enemy advance. He took around ten German officers by surprise at a radio post. He revealed his identity and ordered for them to put their hands up. Startled, some of them immediately obeyed, whilst others tried to reach for their guns. Without hesitating a second, Wray shot them down, unaware that he had just decimated the staff of the *GR. 1058*. Recommended to receive the Medal of Honor, he was finally awarded the DSC.

A GI inspecting the wreck of a Renault UE Chenillette belonging to the French infantry. The outline of a Waco glider can be seen behind the hedge. Twenty-three gliders successfully landed in the immediate vicinity of the village. © NARA

THE MANOIR DE LA FIÈRE

The marshlands in the area obliged the paras from the 505th PIR's A Company to advance along the road leading to the La Fière bridge. By dawn, First Lieutenant John Dolan's group was within 250 metres of its target. Dolan precautiously sent Second Lieutenant Donald G. Coxon from B Company and two pathfinders ahead of the group. With the marshes preventing them from taking to the fields, the Five O'Fivers kept to the road when, suddenly, a machine gun opened fire on them. One man collapsed to the ground. Wounded, Coxon and PVT Ferguson tried to take cover. Hit again in the stomach, the officer died shortly afterwards. The machine gunfire was coming from a manor house where around thirty Germans were entrenched. Second Lieutenant Robert E. McLaughlin, his radio operator and PVT Franck Busa all met with the same fate a few minutes later.

La Fière bridge after the battle. The destroyed German tanks can be seen in the background. © NARA

Without cover, the paras advanced through the ditches. © NARA

I can't estimate how long we were pinned down in this fashion, but it was at least an hour. I made several attempts to move, but drew their fire. On my last attempt, I drew no fire. They obviously had pulled out. During all of this time, I could hear rifle and machine gunfire down by the bridge to the north side. This ceased about the time I returned to the rest of the third Platoon, instructed the Non-Coms to reorganize and to maintain their present position.

First Lieutenant John Dolan, A Company, 505th PIR

Along with Major James E. McGinity, second-in-command of the 1/505 PIR, Dolan tried a bypass manoeuvre. A platoon led by First Lieutenant George W. Presnell was approaching the manor from the north. As they progressed to the south, McGinity's group was spotted by the Germans. The Major was hit by a machine gun. Dolan dived into a ditch and found himself totally isolated.

Around 500 metres to the east, Captain Floyd B. Schwarzwalder was leading 60 paras from the 3/507 PIR on a mission to join Amfreville by crossing the River Merderet. Alerted by the sound of the gunfire, the group moved towards the bridge. First Lieutenant John W. Marr had been stopped in his tracks by gunfire from the manor, along with several paras sent on reconnaissance. Marr informed his superior of the situation before attempting a new approach. A flurry of machine gunfire sent two paras to the ground. Corporal Lawton and PVT Parletto neutralised a machine gun nest with a grenade, yet any further advance remained impossible. Shortly after 9am, Gavin appeared with a group of around 300 men, essentially from the 507th PIR. Lindquist's paras attacked the manor from behind. The paras from A Company persevered. Second Lieutenant William R. Oakley engaged the troops defending the manor to the south, whilst First Lieutenant Presnell's group did likewise to the north. The old fortified property was the theatre of bitter combat. The deployment of a .30 calibre machine gun enabled the Allies to eliminate the German soldiers who were protecting the access to the bridge and the manor.

Although relatively long to set up the M1919 .30 calibre machine gun was an efficient weapon
© Mémorial de Caen collection/Photo C. Prime

Meanwhile, the paras landed to the east of the river joined forces and advanced towards La Fière, following the railway embankment that ran through the marshes. Hence, Colonel Roy E. Lindquist from the 508th PIR and a few elements from the 505th PIR's C Company, commanded by Captain Stefanich, arrived within reach of the manor with around a hundred men. Other groups gradually followed, enabling a concentric attack to be launched on the manor mid morning. The paras from the 505th and 508th PIR thrust forth. Barricaded on the upper floors of the property, the Germans retaliated, but it was too late; the paras had already penetrated inside the courtyard and outbuildings. The Leroux family who owned the manor was found in the cellar. Persistant bazooka fire finally undermined the determination of the last remaining defenders, who surrendered around midday. The Americans could now set foot on the west bank of the Merderet. The parachutists dug out fox holes and set mines. A German truck was pushed onto the middle of a bridge to serve as a barrage. Two bazooka teams were positioned on either side of the bridge parapets.

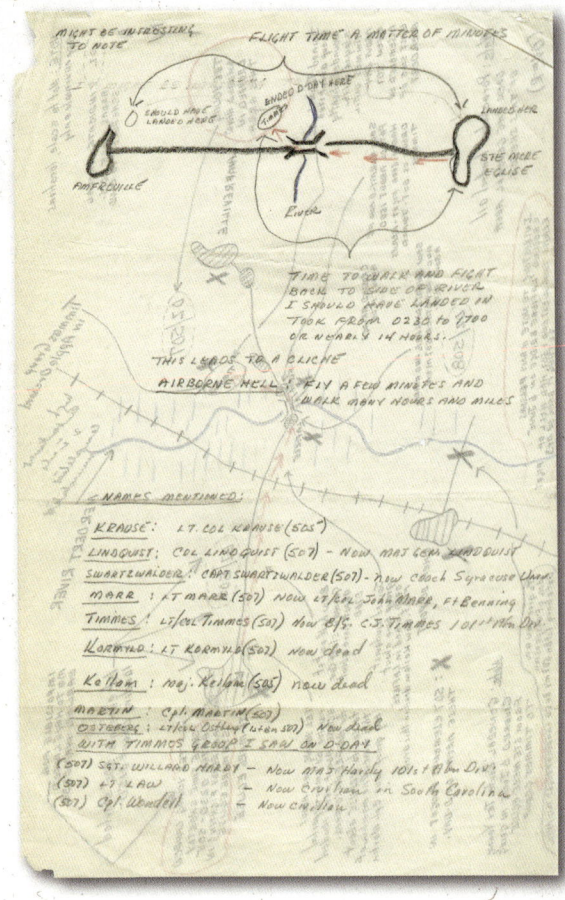

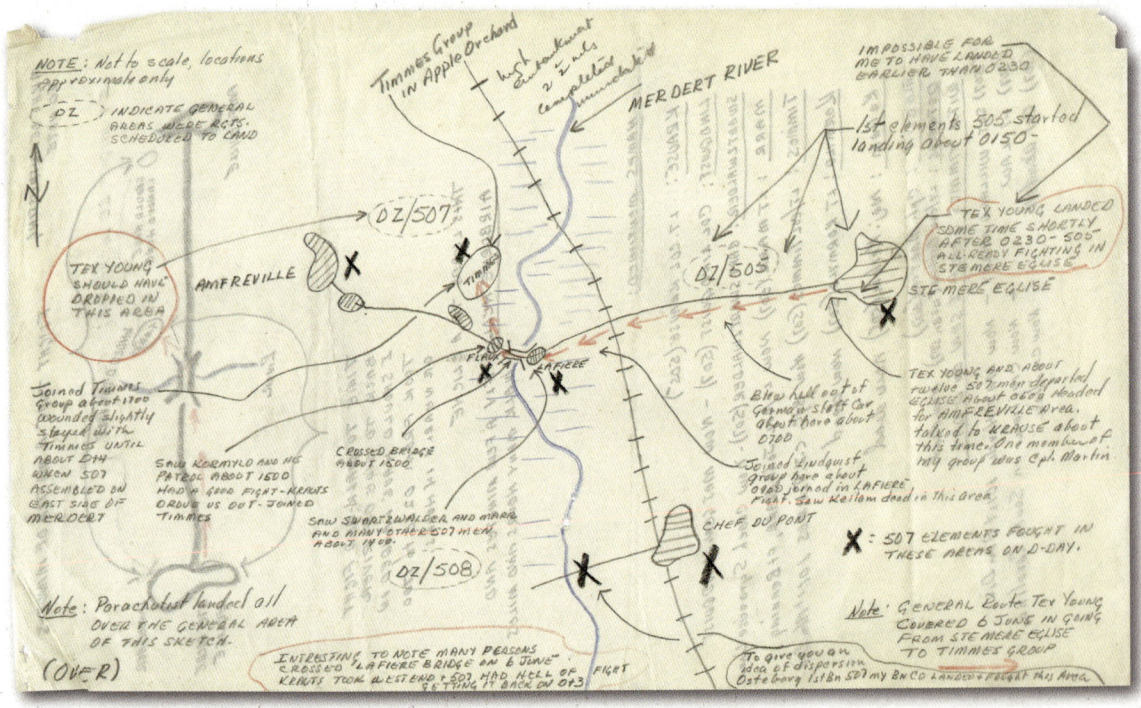

Combat plan for the La Fière sector produced by First Lieutenant Willard Tex Young from the 507th PIR.
© Ohio University Library

AMFREVILLE

To the north-west of La Fière, elements from the 507th PIR continued to fight, despite their isolation. Lieutenant Colonel Charles J. Timmes and thirty paras established a defensive position in an orchard located on the edge of the marshes. The commander of the 2/507 PIR, Colonel George van Millet, who had taken up position in the hamlet of Les Landes, led forty men to engage in combat against the Germans occupying Amfreville. Alerted by the sound of the shooting, Timmes attacked to the east; however, enemy fire was so intense that the U.S. paras were forced into retreat. They surrounded the hamlet, yet failed to take control. Early afternoon, Captain Schwarzwalder's group took to the road to head for Cauquigny, where they found around fifty men from the 507th PIR's D Company. They organised their defensive positions in a small graveyard by the chapel. As they were trying to break through the enemy lines, Millet and several other men were captured on the 8th of June. Timmes held out, successfully establishing contact with the 1/325 GIR, on its way to Amfreville. However, the American attacks were vain and the glider units sustained heavy losses.

A grenadier waiting in ambush and keeping a close watch over the surrounding landscapes thanks to his 6X30 binoculars. Two stick grenades and his Mauser 98K rifle are close at hand. © Private collection

The Germans went to great lengths to keep hold of the hamlet of Cauquigny, the only access route across the marshes to the west. Two glidermen posing in front of the chapel.
© NARA

BENZEDRINE

It is common knowledge that the Germans issued Pervitin, in other words amphetamines, to their soldiers to stimulate them and to reduce the effects of fatigue during combat. The U.S. Army had its own equivalent: Benzedrine Sulfate. The tablets, which were produced by the laboratory Smith, Kline and French, based in Philadelphia, were issued to parachutists. They were to be taken upon orders from their officers in the case of extreme fatigue. To avoid addiction, it was clearly indicated that dosage was to be limited to six tablets per week.

Each box of Benzedrine contained six tablets packaged in a thick paper parcel.
© Private collection

A column of paras walking past a Renault R35 tank as they enter a hamlet. © NARA

La Fière was a sorry sight. Whilst the bodies have been evacuated, the wrecks of four tanks bear witness to the bitter combat here. © NARA

KELLAM BRIDGE

Just a few hundred metres to the east, Lieutenant Colonel Timmes rallied round the paras from the 2/507 PIR and marched to Cauquigny to establish contact with the bridgehead. At midday, the handful of American soldiers in the village were ousted out by grenadiers from the *GR. 1057*. A vast share of the contingent then headed towards Chef-du-Pont to take control of the bridge.

Early afternoon, 200 grenadiers from the *GR. 1057* overwhelmed the paras, isolating Timmes and his men in the process. The Germans accentuated the pressure on the La Fière bridge, which was held by a 505th PIR battalion. At around 4pm, the U.S. paras defending the La Fière position saw them approach, led by a *Panzer III* tank and two R-35 tanks belonging to the *Panzer-Ersatz-Abteilung 100*. The American positions were showered with shells. Major Frederick C. Kellam, commander of the 1/505 PIR, and his second-in-command, Captain Dale A. Roysdon, were killed by a mortar shell as they tried to recover ammunition for the bazookas. Soon, A Company only had fifteen men still fit for combat. The servers of the 57mm antitank gun that was defending the causeway were put out of action after immobilising one of the tanks. Yet, the gun turret relentlessy continued firing on Sergeant Owens and his troopers, condemning them to stay put in their fox hole. At that very moment, PVT Joseph Cyril Fitt from C Company crossed the bridge under a deluge of gunfire, climbed up onto the tank and threw a grenade inside, killing all its occupants. The two bazooka teams from A Company, PFC John D. Bolderson, Leonard Peterson and PVTs. Gordon C, Pryne and Marcus Heim Jr. finally managed to

Panzer III tank tracks. © Private collection

destroy the last two tanks. The arrival of around a hundred men from Chef-du-Pont was to stabilise the situation by evening.

At around 8am on the 7th of June, German mortar shells poured down on Dolan and his men's positions. Two German tanks were advancing towards La Fière. They were stopped by bazooka teams. The German retaliation was instantaneous. A deluge of gunfire showered down on the American positions. Hit by shrapnel, Second Lieutenant Oakley died at the first aid post. Despite a now critical situation for the paras defending the La Fière bridge, Dolan ordered for them to hold out to the bitter end. Then, against all expectations, the Germans asked for a truce in order to evacuate the wounded. The

The locality referred to as 'La Vallée de Misère' (the valley of misery) was the theatre of bitter, and sometimes hand-to-hand combat with blade weapons. As illustrated in this picture, the Germans suffered terrible losses.© NARA

Americans accepted and did likewise. No further frontal enemy attack was launched on the bridge. For their heroic action, Marcus Heim, Leonard Peterson, John Bolderson and Gordon Pryne were decorated with the Distinguished Service Cross.

A para giving some water to a wounded young German soldier who escaped the combat in the 'valley of misery'. © NARA

JOSEPH CYRIL FITT (1924-1944)

Born in Salt Lake City (Utah), Joe Fitt was engaged in the Sicilian and Italian campaigns. Enlisted in the 505th PIR's C Company, he was dropped in the Neuville-au-Plain sector on the night of the 5th to the 6th of June. By 7am, he was in the La Fière sector with 70 other paras from his company. He distinguished himself by neutralising a German tank crew with a grenade. For this feat of arms, he was awarded the Silver Star- sadly posthumously for he was killed on the 13th of June by an isolated sniper near the Montebourg railway station. He is laid to rest at the Taylorsville Memorial Park, in his home in Utah.

Despite his juvenile appearance, Joe Fitt was already a veteran. He took part in operations in Sicily and in Salerno with the 505th PIR's C Company.

© Rights reserved

CHEF-DU-PONT

The 82nd Airborne Division's second mission was to take control of the Chef-du-Pont and La Fière bridges over the River Merderet, in order to establish a bridgehead to the west of the marshes.

The Chef-du-Pont bridge was entrusted to the 1/505 PIR; however, since Major Kellam had only successfully reunited a small share of his unit, he decided to head for La Fière.

Gavin ordered for Lieutenant Colonel Arthur A. Maloney's 3/507 PIR to find another bridge enabling the Merderet to be crossed. The latter immediately obeyed orders, setting off with 75 men. A little later, the second-in-command of the 82nd Airborne Division was informed that Chef-du-Pont was the site of very little, if not no German defence. He immediately despatched Lieutenant Colonel Edwin J. Ostberg's 1/507 PIR to seize the target. With around a hundred men, the officer entered the locality mid morning. The houses had been cleared;

Troopers and gliders from the 82nd Airborne Division exchanging a few words at a crossroads leading to Chef-du-Pont.
© NARA

however, the solidly entrenched Germans from *GR. 1058* stopped the American troops' progression around 400 metres from the bridge. Ostberg was wounded in the very first minutes. A gun positioned on the right bank caused minor losses in the American ranks.

Both sides received reinforcements and intense close-range combat ensued. Alerted by the noise of the battle, Maloney adopted a hastier pace to lend a hand, but finally received orders from Gavin to head for La Fière. Thirty-four paras from E Company finally managed to come within reach of the oh-so coveted bridge. After an ultimate counter-attack aimed at ousting them out, the Germans withdrew by night towards Carquebut. Fighting was particularly fierce. The providential landing of a glider transporting a gun and ammunition, combined with the arrival of around 30 infantrymen from the 8th U.S. Infantry Regiment enabled the Americans to secure the sector.

On many pictures, the paras show their war spoils. Hence, this bust dons a Walther P-38 pistol a *Heer* ammunition belt and a pair of 6x30 binoculars.
© Mémorial de Caen collection/Photo C. Prime

These German soldiers have set up their MG 42 machine gun on its Lafette mount behind a thick hedgerow. They have covered their helmets with fragments of camouflaged parachute canopy. © Private collection

LA RAFF FORCE

Lieutenant-Colonel Walter F. Winton was sent to join forces with the reinforcements landed by sea. He informed Ridgway that elements from the 4th U.S. Infantry Division were advancing around the hamlet of Les Forges, just a few kilometres to the south of Sainte-Mère, with the mission to take control of the ridge at Fauville-Turqueville, still in enemy hands. Winton also established contact with the freshly landed seaborne elements from the Howell Force.

Colonel Edson Raff from the 507th PIR had been chosen by Ridgway to lead a small mechanised force that was to land on Utah Beach. Although this appointment may appear as a vexatious measure against an experienced parachute officer who demonstrated very little respect for his chief, the mission entrusted to the Raff Force remained vital: to secure LZ W and to reach Sainte-Mère as quickly as possible. The force was composed of a company from the 325th GIR, 17 Sherman tanks from the 746th Tank Battalion's C Company and four M8 Greyhound Light Armoured Cars from the 4th Cavalry Squadron. The armoured column left Utah at 2pm to reach the Les Forges junction unhindered.

Photographs of Ridgway in Normandy are quite a rarity. This one was taken by the La Couture farm. © NARA

Paras from Force C, landed by sea, walking through Sainte-Marie-du-Mont on their way to Les Forges.
© NARA

A column marching past a destroyed Sherman belonging to the 746th Tank Battalion. © Medusky collection

At this precise moment, the German 88mm gun fired and hit the lead tanks. Three tanks were destroyed, one after another. The Americans immediately retaliated, sending a deluge of shellfire showering down onto Hill 20. The column resumed its advance, taking a detour through the village of Chef-du-Pont. Colonel Raff entered the La Couture farm located 2km to the west of Sainte-Mère-Église, to find dozens of wounded soldiers lying on the ground, agonising and groaning, together with German prisoners watched over by wounded paras. Sainte-Mère's local GP, Dr Rivière, rushed to take care of the most seriously wounded, with help from Mme Pesnel and her daughter. The practitioner informed the American officer that Ridgway and his staff had set up headquarters on the opposite side of the farm courtyard. The armoured column stopped for the night. With the Germans still in control of the sector around Les Forges and Fauville, LZ W remained totally isolated.

The BC611 Handie Talkie was one of the best means of communication for the airborne troops. © Private collection

THE ARRIVAL OF REINFORCEMENTS

At 9pm on the 6th of June, 140 Horsa and 36 Waco gliders were to land in four successive waves on LZ W, with some 1,190 men from the 82nd Airborne Division, 67 jeeps, 24 howitzers (105mm and 75mm), 13 antitank guns and 55 tonnes of equipment on board.

Mission Elmira was a risky enterprise for the drop zone was still threatened by Germans, entrenched in the hamlets of Turqueville and Fauville. Duly informed, Ridgway tried, in vain, to alert the airborne formations to reroute to LZ O. The gliders became easy targets during their approach.

LZ W stretched across a length of 2,000 metres and a width of 1,500 metres; but it was far from a simple task for pilots to land their craft in the dark in such a small perimeter of fields edged with hedges and high poplars, as is the case in this part of Normandy. The gliders also had trouble braking on the damp grass. Their wooden and canvas structures smashed into the embankments and other obstacles.

Several gliders crashed to the ground. Small groups of German soldiers infiltrated the landing zone and opened fire on the gliders. The pilots, who had undergone intensive training, retaliated like simple infantrymen. One pilot and a few glidermen were dragging the wounded out of the fuselage of a Horsa riddled with bullet holes, when they were struck down by automatic guns, before being able to take shelter. The German soldiers approached and finished off the remaining wounded, lying under one of the wings. The wounded pilot hid under the bodies, only to be rescued the following day. Heavy losses were sustained. No less than 227 men, among whom 26 pilots, were killed or wounded. One C-47 and five gliders were destroyed, 92 others seriously damaged.

This sad toll led to a change in itinerary for missions Galveston and Hackensack, launched the following morning and directed above the Douve valley, in order to avoid the Flak. LZ E, the less exposed of the landing zones, was the new chosen site. At 6.55am, a hundred C-47 Skytrains, towing 18 Horsa and 82 Waco gliders (two were forced to make a u-turn) transported Lieutenant Colonel Klemm R. Boyd's

C-47s from the 88th TCS, towing Waco gliders, flew over the flooded area inland from Utah Beach to head for LZ W. They were transporting elements from the 82nd Airborne Division taking part in mission Elmira. © USAAF

On the 7th of June, the gliders began their descent towards LZ E in Hiesville. The presence of tanks on the road suggests that the zone has been secured. © NARA

The flight of one Horsa ended in a brick wall behind the hospice to the north of Sainte-Mère. The front of the craft literally disintegrated under the violence of the impact. © NARA

Waco CG-4 glider tow line
© Vassas collection/Photo C. Prime

1/526 GIR and the rest of the division's artillery, i.e. some 927 men, 20 artillery pieces and 41 vehicles. Twenty-six aircraft were damaged and 17 glidermen were killed during mission Elmira.

At 8.51am, the first formation of 30 Horsa and 20 Waco gliders transporting the 3/325 GIR and 2/401 GIR landed in the fields around LZ W, already scattered with the wrecks of several aircraft. One glider was shot down, fifteen men were killed and sixty others wounded. One last series of fifty Waco gliders sustained minor losses while transporting service troops, 81mm mortars and a company from the 401st GIR to LZ W. Due to the lack of pilots and gliders, several hundreds of glider units were brought in by boat over the afternoon. The 325th GIR had successfully rallied 90% of its available forces.

Paras hastily fleeing the fuselage of a Horsa glider. © NARA

THE AIRSPEED HORSA GLIDER

The Airspeed Horsa, designed by the engineer Hessell Tiltman, was built entirely of wood, which meant it could be produced in converted furniture factories. Its cylindrical fuselage could accommodate 28 fully equipped men, seated on benches. The craft was loaded via sliding doors to the rear and the front left. Its tricycle undercarriage was jettisoned during the flight and landing was made using a sprung skid on the underside of the fuselage. The reinforced floor of the Horsa Mk. II meant it could transport a light vehicle. When loaded, the glider weighed in at nearly 7 tonnes. To facilitate unloading operations, its tail could be severed from the fuselage.

SECURING THE BRIDGEHEAD AT THE MERDERET

The arrival of reinforcements enabled the commander of the 82nd U.S. Airborne Division to launch a counter-attack to the north, aimed at permanently securing the airborne bridgehead. Vandervoort was entrusted with the mission of advancing along the RN13 trunk road, with support from tanks from the 746th Tank Battalion. First Lieutenant Peterson's paras began marching at 5.15pm. The American tanks defied the *Panzerjäger 709* assault guns. Paras and grenadiers ended up engaging in hand-to-hand combat. The German line of defence was broken through: 4 German tanks were annihilated; 150 soldiers were killed or wounded and at least 700 taken prisoner. The Germans retreated to Montebourg.

To the south, the 4th U.S. Infantry Division's 8th Infantry Regiment was given a rough time by the *Ost-Bataillon 795*, entrenched in the hamlets of Ecausseville, Écoquenéauville and Turqueville. Finally, Colonel Neely's 2nd Battalion successfully reached Sainte-Mère-Église, much to the relief of the paras from the 505th PIR.

Having already lost 160 men in the Les Forges sector, the 325th GIR was engaged without delay. Colonel Lewis immediately despatched three battalions to Chef-du-Pont and Carquebut. Both sites having been cleared of any enemy presence, the regiment was sent to Sainte-Mère and La Fière. Meanwhile, the 1/325 moved northwards along the railway line embankment. It was then to cross a narrow river to take the German positions defending the bridge from the rear, then to join forces with Colonel Timmes with whom initial contact had been established. The discovery of a submerged passageway through the Merderet marshes enabled the glider troops to infiltrate the sector. Colonel Millet's group from the 507th PIR headed towards Amfreville. It was dispersed by a violent attack on the night of the 8th to 9th of June.

The 1/325 GIR received orders to cross the Merderet to the north of La Fière and to secure the roadway to join forces with the parachutists entrenched in the locality of Les Landes and with Lieutenant Colonel Timmes' group to the east of Amfreville. Meanwhile, Millet was to progress eastwards to join the American lines. However, Millet was captured with several of his men. The German resistance proved to be such that the attack on La Fière led by Major Sanford's glidermen was forced into retreat.

CHARLES N. DEGLOPPER (1921-1944)

Enlisted in November 1942, DeGlopper integrated the airlanded infantry, to be affected to the 325th GIR's C Company. On the 7th of June, his battalion was brought in by glider and sent towards the La Fière road. As it was marching towards its target, his company fell into an ambush by the hamlet of Le Motey. DeGlopper volunteered to cover his retreating buddies with his Browning automatic rifle. He advanced, uncovered, along the road, drawing enemy gunfire. He was hit several times before taking to his knees. Demonstrating exemplary bravery and abnegation, he continued to retaliate before being killed by an enemy bullet. This exceptional feat of arms earned DeGlopper the posthumous award of the Medal of Honor.

DeGlopper was a sturdy soldier measuring almost two metres.
© Rights reserved

Gliders have installed a .30 calibre machine gun in a gap in a hedge. © NARA

Lewis received orders from Gavin to launch a new attack towards Amfreville. Given the reluctance of Lieutenant Colonel Carrel to lead this action, he was immediately replaced by Major Gardner. Preceded by an artillery barrage, the battalion thrust forth towards the bridge, covered by the guns of their fellow parachutists from the 507th PIR and the Sherman tanks positioned at the La Fière Manor. But the Germans had not said their last word. Their mortars and machine guns decimated the glider troops. The road was soon scattered with the dead and wounded. One tank drove over a mine, exploded and crashed into the wreck of a German tank, blocking the passageway. The survivors crawled along the ditches. To the west, the situation was critical for Timmes' Raff's Ruffians. German shells showered down on their beseiged positions. PVT Joe Gandara from D Company came out of

Browning Automatic Rifle (BAR). © Rights reserved

The 307th Airborne Medical Company established an advanced first aid post at the La Couture farm, which was also home to Ridgway's command post. © NARA

© Rights reserved

his fox hole with a .30 caliber gun and neutralised three enemy positions before collapsing, mortally wounded. He was awarded the Distinguished Service Cross (and the Medal of Honor in 2014).

Gavin decided to send his paras back into the fray. Captain Rae and his men returned up the 500 metres of roadway, galvanising the gliders, lying on the ground along the emblankment, yet deemed still fit for combat. This time, the Germans failed to push back the All Americans' ultimate thrust. Cauquigny was theirs. Rae continued his momentum as far as the hamlet of Le Motey to the south of Amfreville, whilst First Lieutenant Stanley Ardziejewski's section established contact with Timmes and his men, entrenched to the east of Amfreville. The 746th Tank Battalion arrived to reinforce the formation. Ridgway's men had fought tooth and nail to secure the bridges of La Fière and Chef-du-Pont, hitherto held by the *91. LLD*.

After relieving the 82nd Airborne Division, depleted and exhausted, the 90th U.S. Infantry Division resumed the attack the following day. But by nightfall, the situation had barely improved, with a toll of 200 men killed and 500 wounded.

Colonel Lewis, in command of the 325th GIR, taking stock of the situation by an 81mm mortar position. © NARA

This young parachutist is enjoying a well-deserved rest on a pile of rubble. © Magnum Photo

American nurse's kit and part of its contents. © Private collection

CUTTING THE PENINSULA

Captain Kenneth L. Johnson from the 508th PIR HQ Company talking with two French civilians. This picture was published in a number of American newspapers. © NARA

The Battle of Normandy was not yet over for the division. Indeed, on the 8th of June, the 505th PIR and a battalion from the 2/325 GIR launched a new attack on Neuville-au-Plain. Combat eventually got the better of the German defenders' determination and they abandoned the small town over the afternoon. The Americans continued their advance to Grainville, by now deserted. The following day, they received orders to take control of a hill located between the railway station in Montebourg and Le Ham. With support from tactical aviation and artillery, the 1/505th PIR reached the station, obliging the Germans to retreat towards Le Ham. In contrast, the 2/325th GIR was at a standstill and remained so until dusk.

On the morning of the 10th of June, the 505th PIR troopers crossed the railway track and advanced, their rifles fitted with bayonets, amidst the marshes, covered by a thick artificial smokescreen.

Gammon No. 82 grenade, much appreciated by the paras for its simple use and the possibility to adapt the explosive charge to suit the target.
© Private collection

However, the Germans continued to fire at random, inflicting severe losses among their adversaries, who were advancing without the slightest cover. Through their unyielding tenacity, the All Americans managed to come within reach of Montebourg, which was occupied by the 8th Infantry Regiment in the evening. Yet, Ridgway's troopers' and gliders' troubles were not over yet. The First U.S. Army decided to divert its line of progression towards the western coast of the Cotentin peninsula, in order to prevent the Germans from reinforcing Cherbourg. The 9th and 90th U.S. Infantry Divisons were on the front lines. The latter was to pave the way for Ridgway's paras at the onset of the attack, before rerouting its march to hold the north flank.

The glider troops from the 325th GIR covered the Tough Ombres to the rear, as the latter broke through the front by Le Motey and Chef-du-Pont. The 508th PIR's mission was to secure the sector between the River Douve and the Gorges marshes, before moving on towards Baupte to join forces with the 101st Airborne Division. The paras destroyed a dozen tanks with a bazooka, only to meet with steadfast resistance a little later, by Houtteville. They were stopped in their tracks by an enemy infantry battalion, and Flak and artillery pieces. Two tanks were destroyed thanks to Gammon grenades. They continued to fight relentlessly throughout the day, in an effort to break through the enemy defences. Baupte finally fell into Allied hands on the 14th.

After a lull, the offensive was resumed. The troopers from the 507th PIR and the gliders from the 325th GIR attacked along the Pont l'Abbé to

A group of paras and gliders after the combat to take Saint-Sauveur-le-Vicomte. © NARA

Paras from the 508th PIR making their way through Saint-Marcouf. This black-faced Technical Sergeant is sitting on the rubble, suggesting the sector is now calm. Yet, some of his men are still on the alert, well-concealed amidst the hedgerows.
© NARA

Saint-Sauveur-le-Vicomte road, whilst the 9th U.S. Infantry Division's Old Reliables covered them to the north.

The parachutist battalions advanced westwards in columns to reach the hamlet of La Bonneville. With armoured support, the 325th GIR deeply penetrated the enemy lines, provoking the premature collapse of the German front. The airlanded infantry troops reached Rauville-la-Place, less than a kilometre from Saint-Sauveur-le-Vicomte. The 505th PIR, which had relieved the 508th, in turn reached Reigneville by dusk. The gliders successfully managed to put the enemy troops to rout the following day. From the left bank of the Douve, the Americans observed the Germans as they left Saint-Sauveur. The latter were seeking to establish a new line of defence slightly further east in order to keep a corridor open to access the peninsula. Ridgway convinced General Collins to allow for the waterway to be crossed in order to establish a bridgehead and to capture the town. The same day, the All Americans crossed the river and formed a 3 kilometre-deep bridgehead. The 9th U.S. Infantry Division crossed the bridgehead held by the paras to head for Barneville, hence isolating the north of the peninsula.

The Garand M1 semi-automatic rifle was a precious ally.
© NARA

Nurses tending to a young boy who has been wounded in the legs and right hand. © NARA

THE CAPTURE OF SAINT-SAUVEUR-LE-VICOMTE

This photo report, taken on the 16th of June during the capture of Saint-Sauveur-le-Vicomte fully illustrates the violence of the combat involved. © Magnum Photo

Lieutenant Colonel Vandervoort and a group of paras in the ruins of the village. © NARA

TOWARDS MONT ÉTENCLIN

Picture of First Lieutenant Kelso Crowder Horne from the 3/508 PIR, several days after the capture of La Fière, taken by the photographer Bob Landry. This remarkable photograph made the front page of Life magazine's 4 August 1944 issue. The officer was seriously wounded on the 4th of July 1944 during the assault on the Sainte-Catherine hill (Hill 95). © Life

© Rights reserved

131) over the morning, to capture 150 Russian and German soldiers. The 508th PIR met with equal success on the south-east slope. In control of the height late afternoon, the Americans then liberated Neufmesnil. The 325th GIR in turn slipped its way alongside the enemy lines to come face to face with the front line. The gliders were stopped in their tracks by the hamlet of La Poterie.

The following day, Ridgway's men attacked the La Poterie ridge, in particular Hill 95 (Sainte-Catherine) located to the east. Battered by several weeks of combat, the units nevertheless thrust towards the heights held by the *353. Infanterie-Division*, under an avalanche of shellfire. The United States of America's Independence Day took on a somewhat bitter taste for these paras, trapped under a barrage of unyielding automatic weapons and mortars. In just 45 minutes, the 508th PIR's H Company lost fifty men. Initially forced to retreat, they nevertheless held strong. The 2/508 PIR took control of the summit at 12.20pm, at a cost of massive losses. However, the next morning,

The unit was then transferred to Beuzeville-la-Bastille, further west. It maintained pressure on the front lines which the enemy had, by now, efficiently reinforced After the capture of Cherbourg on the 26th of June, the U.S. high command decided to advance southwards. On the 3rd of July, the VIII Corps engaged in combat in the sector of La Haye-du-Puits.

The troopers left Prétot under pouring rain to rapidly neutralise the enemy's front-line positions. A company from the 505th PIR, guided by a young Norman, managed to make its way across the north slope of Mont Étenclin (Hill

the German infantry counter-attacked, forcing the Americans off the position. The hill was conquered once more on the 7th of July by the Red Devils, then again by the 1/325 GIR the following day. The 507th PIR also reached the top of the neighbouring hill, but the parachutists were to engage in fierce hand-to-hand combat in order to maintain their positions. The 505th PIR encountered less difficult terrain.

Whilst Major General Ridgway's men could be rightly proud of having reached all their targets, these last days of combat had bled dry this division that had been deprived of any reinforcement since the 6th of June. The 82nd Airborne Division was removed from the front pending its transfer to England. After a few days of well-deserved rest, the men headed for Utah Beach on the 12th of July, where they boarded the two Landing Ships that took them back to Southampton.

In 27 days of combat, the division had demonstrated its valiance and its strength, but at a cost of terrible losses. A later report established that it had lost a total of 5,436 men, among whom 1,142 dead, i.e. 45% of its total force.

Gliders firing from behind a hedge. © NARA

Thirty-three days of action without relief, without replacements. Every mission accomplished. No ground gained was ever relinquished.

Major General Ridgway

Late July, Lieutenant General Omar Bradley decorated the paras and the gliders from the 82nd U.S. Airborne Division who had distinguished themselves during the battle of Sainte-Mère-Église. Gavin (absent on this picture), Krause and Vandervoort, with his walking stick, received the Distinguished Service Cross. © NARA

Private Elmet Habbs taking a rest at the foot of the sign at the entrance to the village of Sainte-Mère. © NARA

CHAPTER 5

AFTER THE BATTLE

SAINTE-MÈRE

Whilst the paras had received orders not to encumber themselves with enemy prisoners or wounded soldiers over the early hours immediately after the Landings, they were later to be taken charge of in abidance by the rules set forth in the Geneva Convention, signed by both countries. © NARA

As the combat zones became increasingly distant, the time had come for people of Sainte-Mère-Église and the airborne troops to bury their dead. The 307th Airborne Medical Company set up a position to the south of Sainte-Mère, not only to care for the division's wounded, but also those from enemy units. On the 18th of June, the 96th Evacuation Hospital was established in the fields to the west of the village. A total of 4,000 patients were treated there, and 2,700 surgical procedures performed.

The village became a crucial communication hub for the U.S. Army, with an endless ebb and flow of soldiers and vehicles to and from Utah Beach over five whole months.

The area around the village was rapidly inundated with individual graves and small military cemeteries where American and German soldiers were buried. The services in charge of burials later decided to reunite them in larger, yet still temporary cemeteries in order to offer them a worthy and respectable place of rest.

Medic armband and box of morphine syrettes.
© Airborne Museum

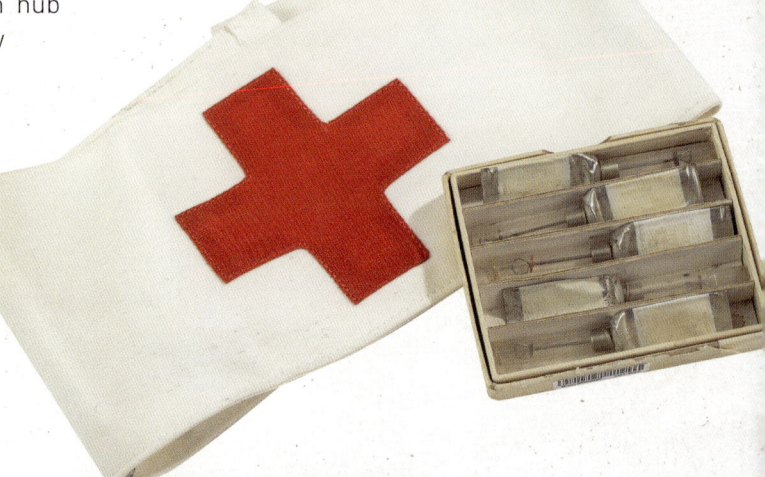

The 603rd Quartermaster Graves Registration Company chose Sainte-Mère-Église to host the first of these resting grounds thanks to its central location and the presence of field hospitals. A plot of land was chosen in the vicinity of the village graveyard.

Hence, Temporary Cemetery No. 1 was created from the 9th to the 11th of June 1944. With help from German POWs and local civilians, the American troops worked relentlessly to bury the 2,195 American and 1,000 German soldiers killed in combat. On the 25th of June, when the site's maximum capacity had been reached, it was decided to create a second cemetery on the western extremity of the village to bury the 4,798 dead from the VII U.S. Corps. Three kilometres from there, the commune of Carquebut (Blosville) was home to a third cemetery with 5,804 graves. Due to the proximity of these three cemeteries, the inhabitants of Sainte-Mère and the surrounding countryside fully grasped the sheer violence of the combat that had been engaged as they watched trucks laden with bodies pass by, and the ever-increasing number of white crosses. They regularly paid visits to the graves to grieve and honour their liberators. Some offered their time to help find and gather the bodies.

Early August 1944, the Americans were greatly moved by a picture published in Life magazine's 7th August 1944 issue of Simone Renaud, the wife of the mayor of Sainte-Mère-Église, placing flowers on the grave of Brigadier General Theodore Roosevelt, the 26th President of the United States' eldest son. She personified this blood tie between the small commune and the United States of America. Throughout her life, Simone Renaud pursued her correspondence with any American families seeking information on the resting place of their family members.

Military chaplain's helmet.
© Airborne Museum

The bodies of killed soldiers were swathed in parachute canopies then buried. © NARA

Each coffin was covered with a 48-star burial flag measuring 1.52m by 2.74m.
© Airborne Museum

Simone Renaud placing flowers on the grave of one of the liberators. The mayor's wife, who spoke and wrote fluent English, took time and care to reply to any American families wishing to be informed of the sites of their loved ones' graves. © Rights reserved

THE 82ND AIRBORNE DIVISION IN THE NETHERLANDS...

All Americans attentively listening to their officer before boarding. Some were preparing to make their fourth operational jump.
© NARA

After healing its wounds and restaffing its ranks with new recruits from the United States, the division resumed training. Ridgway, who had been appointed commander of the XVIII Airborne Corps, was replaced by Gavin, who was promoted to the grade of Major General, becoming the youngest ever commander of a division since the American Civil War. The force was also reorganised. The 504th PIR replaced the 507th which joined the 17th U.S. Airborne Division.

The All Americans were placed on the alert. They were to take part in operation Market Garden, aimed at enabling the Allies to penetrate the very heart of Germany, via Holland. The 82nd and the 101st Airborne Divisions, together with the 1st British Airborne Division were entrusted with the mission of paving the way for the XXX British Corps tanks, by taking control of several bridges over the rivers and canals leading to Arnhem.

On the 17th of September 1944, the 7,277 paras were dropped shortly before 1pm to the south of the town of Nijmegen, to take possession of the bridges over the Meuse, the Waal and the canal linking the two rivers together. The drop zones were rapidly secured. Fifty Waco gliders airlanded 209 glider troops and the necessary heavy equipment. Bad weather prevented the rest of the 325th GIR from being brought in. The Heuman bridge fell intact into the hands of the 504th PIR; however, the paras failed to prevent the destruction of the bridges over the Maas-Waal canal.

Brigadier General Gavin's M1 helmet. As well as the two stars, the insignia of the VII Corps have been welded to the sides. © Airborne Museum

JAMES GAVIN

From a modest Brooklyn family, James Gavin enlisted in the U.S. Army at the age of 18 and trained at Fort Sherman in Panama. Through his hard work, the young man successfully integrated the United States Military Academy at West Point in 1924, from which he graduated five years later. He was affected to the 25th Infantry Regiment before joining the Fort Benning Infantry School. With no desire to become an instructor, Gavin then joined the 28th and 29th Infantry Regiments. After spending eighteen months in the Philippines, he served in the 3rd U.S. Infantry Division and was promoted to the grade of Captain. Having acquired a particular interest in the development of the airborne army, Gavin integrated the Fort Benning Airborne School in July 1941. He took command of the 505th PIR in August 1942 and shaped the regiment in his own fashion. And he led it into combat both in Sicily and in Normandy. At the age of 36, Gavin was promoted to the grade of Brigadier General on the 10th of October 1943, making him the youngest General in the U.S. Army. During operation Market Garden, he fractured a disc during a jump, but said nothing, and continued to fight for around two months, regardless. He took command of the division during the Battle of the Bulge, leading his men into Berlin. He retired from the army in March 1958 as Lieutenant General, and joined a consultancy firm of which he became the director. Slim Jim died on the 23rd of February 1990. He is laid to rest in the old chapel at the United States Military Academy at West Point.

James Gavin was nicknamed 'Slim Jim' due to his slender build. © NARA

The 505th PIR took up cover positions to the south of Groesbeek, while the 508th PIR advanced towards Nijmegen.

Unfortunately, the regiment failed to take the bridge, which was defended by a *10. SS-Panzer-Division Frundsberg* reconnaisance battalion.

The following day, the regiment retreated to the drop zones, which were equally threatened. Joined on the 19th of September by the Guards Armoured Division, the division tried once more to take the Nijmegen bridge, but, despite the added support from the tanks, its efforts were in vain. On the 20th, the paras had further German attacks to defy by Groesbeek. The 3/504 PIR crossed the Waal aboard small boats, under hails of shellfire and mortar: 26 vessels sank and 200 men were unfit for combat. However, the German defenders found themselves sandwiched between the U.S. units and were forced to abandon the bridge. This operation had proved to be very costly for the All Americans: 469 killed, 1,933 wounded and 640 unaccounted for.

For operation Market Garden, the paras exchanged their M-42 uniforms for the new M43 model. © NARA

The Dutch people extended a hearty welcome to the men from the 82nd Airborne Division. © NARA

Drops were made by day, in full view of the Germans. © NARA

Three troopers posing in front of the bridge over the River Waal. Three wounded German soldiers are lying in front of them. © NARA

... IN THE HEART OF GERMANY

The unit occupied defensive positions in the Netherlands up to the 11th of November, the day the men headed for Reims to rest and to replace the missing ranks. However, the onset of the German offensive in the Ardennes on the 16th of December was to curtail this well-deserved period of respite. The division immediately got on its way. Deployed in the Stavelot sector, along the line of advance of three *Waffen-SS* armoured divisions, it contributed towards the destruction of the *Kampfgruppe Peiper*, yet failed to contain the *Panzer* attacks by the *Das Reich* and *LAH* divisions. The troopers and gliders duly withdrew along the line running from Manhay to Trois-Ponts, continuing to fight to the bitter end.

On the 3rd of January 1945, Gavin's division took part in the Allied counter-attack aimed at regaining the lost ground. In just a month, around 2,700 men were put out of action. Some of the division's soldiers distinguished themselves once more. Still on the front lines, Vandervoort was wounded in the shoulder and lost his left eye as he led the assault on Goronne on the 7th of January. First Sergeant Leonard Funck from the 508th PIR was awarded the Medal of Honor for having successfully controlled a column of German prisoners who had just disarmed their guards.

The division fought in the Ruhr before heading back to Reims mid-February 1945. Just like their buddies from the 101st Airborne Division, the All Americans were not part of operation Varsity. In March, they were sent to Bonn, before occupying the left bank of the Elbe, by Cologne.

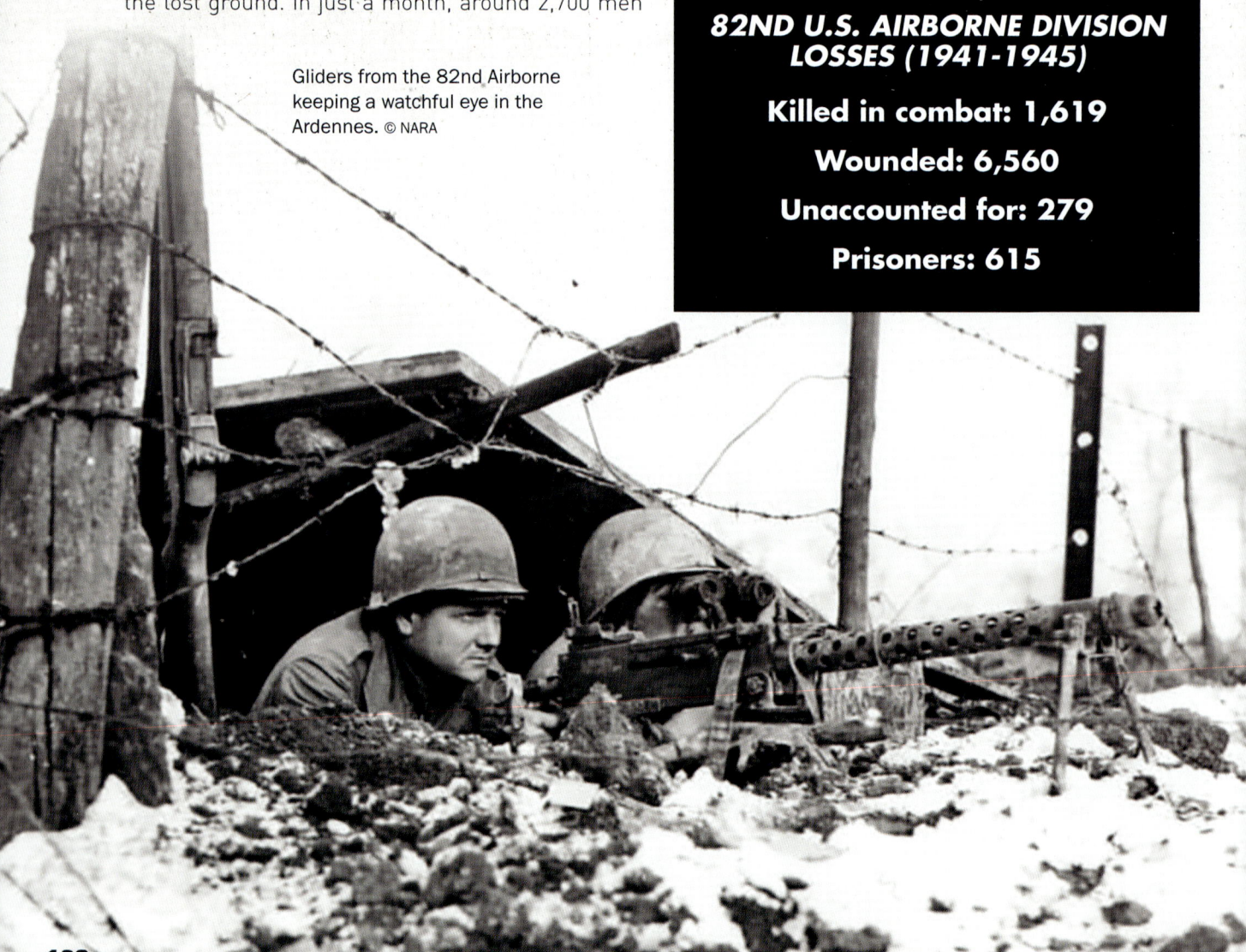

Gliders from the 82nd Airborne keeping a watchful eye in the Ardennes. © NARA

82ND U.S. AIRBORNE DIVISION LOSSES (1941-1945)

Killed in combat: 1,619

Wounded: 6,560

Unaccounted for: 279

Prisoners: 615

In front of Cologne Cathedral, Corporal Luther E. Boger from the 82nd Airborne Division reading a sign warning 'sight seers' to respect this limit to avoid friendly fire. © NARA

The division was then sent to northern Germany. After crossing the Elbe, it obtained the surrender of the *21. Armee* in Ludwigslust, before joining the Red Army on the 3rd of May. The previous day, in collaboration with the 8th U.S. Infantry Division, it had liberated the Wöbbelin subcamp, part of the Neuengamme concentration camp. The interior courtyard was scattered with the bodies of a thousand prisoners. The next day, as per Eisenhower's orders, the inhabitants of Ludwigslust were requisitioned to visit the camp and bury the dead. A funeral service was organised three days later. Several hundreds of men from the division attended.

The 82nd Airborne Division was sent to Berlin with the distinct honour of acting as the town's guard of honour before heading back to France, to Auxerre, to be demobilised on the 30th of November 1945.

This new campaign was an ordeal for those who had not been issued with winter clothing. Most often, they only had linen drape greatcoats to wear over their M43 uniforms. © NARA

The All Americans fraternising with Uncle Joe's (Stalin) combattants.
© NARA

SAINTE-MÈRE-ÉGLISE'S POSTERITY

During commemorative ceremonies, the local youngsters are delighted to dress up as paras, much to the delight of visiting U.S. veterans. © NARA

The summer of 1948 marked the closure of the temporary cemeteries and the transfer of lost troops towards the permanent cemetery in Saint-Laurent-sur-Mer, a heartbreaking experience for the local population. The loyal commitment of the mayor Alexandre Renaud and his wife failed to convince the American Battle Monument Commission.

Yet the profound link that unites the village with its liberators is such that members of the 82nd Airborne returned to the spot as early as 1945, hence contributing towards the posterity of Sainte-Mère. In December 1947, the town of Locust Valley, in the State of New York, participated in the village's reconstruction, in complement to the Marshall plan, during operation Democracy.

The village of Sainte-Mère organised a celebration in commemoration of the first anniversary of the 1945 liberation. At the time posted in Berlin, the division sent thirty men to take part. Later, generals were officially invited to attend commemorations: Eisenhower (1951), Ridgway (1952), Gavin (1962) and Bradley (1974).
© NARA

Eighteen years after the D-Day Landings, another event contributed towards its international renown. The film *The Longest Day*, by the American film director Darryl Francis Zanuck, was released. This war film, inspired by the eponymous best-selling book by Cornelius Ryan, published in 1959, met with tremendous success with over 12 million spectators. The film's emblematic scene is undoubtedly the one when the paras are dropped on the village square in Sainte-Mère-Église, and more specifically portraying the unfortunate 'landing' by John Steele from the 2/505 PIR (played by the actor Red Buttons) on the church spire, where he remained for several hours. The film was awarded two Oscars and one Golden Globe. To this very day, a trip to Sainte-Mère to see the dummy parachutist still hanging from the church spire is one of the must-do events to add to any tour of Normandy's battlefields.

Photograph of the two temporary cemeteries set up near Sainte-Mère-Église. Each grave bore a plaque with the soldier's name. © Rights Reserved/Airborne Museum

John Wayne, who played Lieutenant Colonel Vandervoort, refused to come to France to film the outdoor scenes of the film *The Longest Day*. © Rights reserved

Red Buttons, alias John Steele was as yet unaware that he would help the village's name to go down in history. © Rights reserved

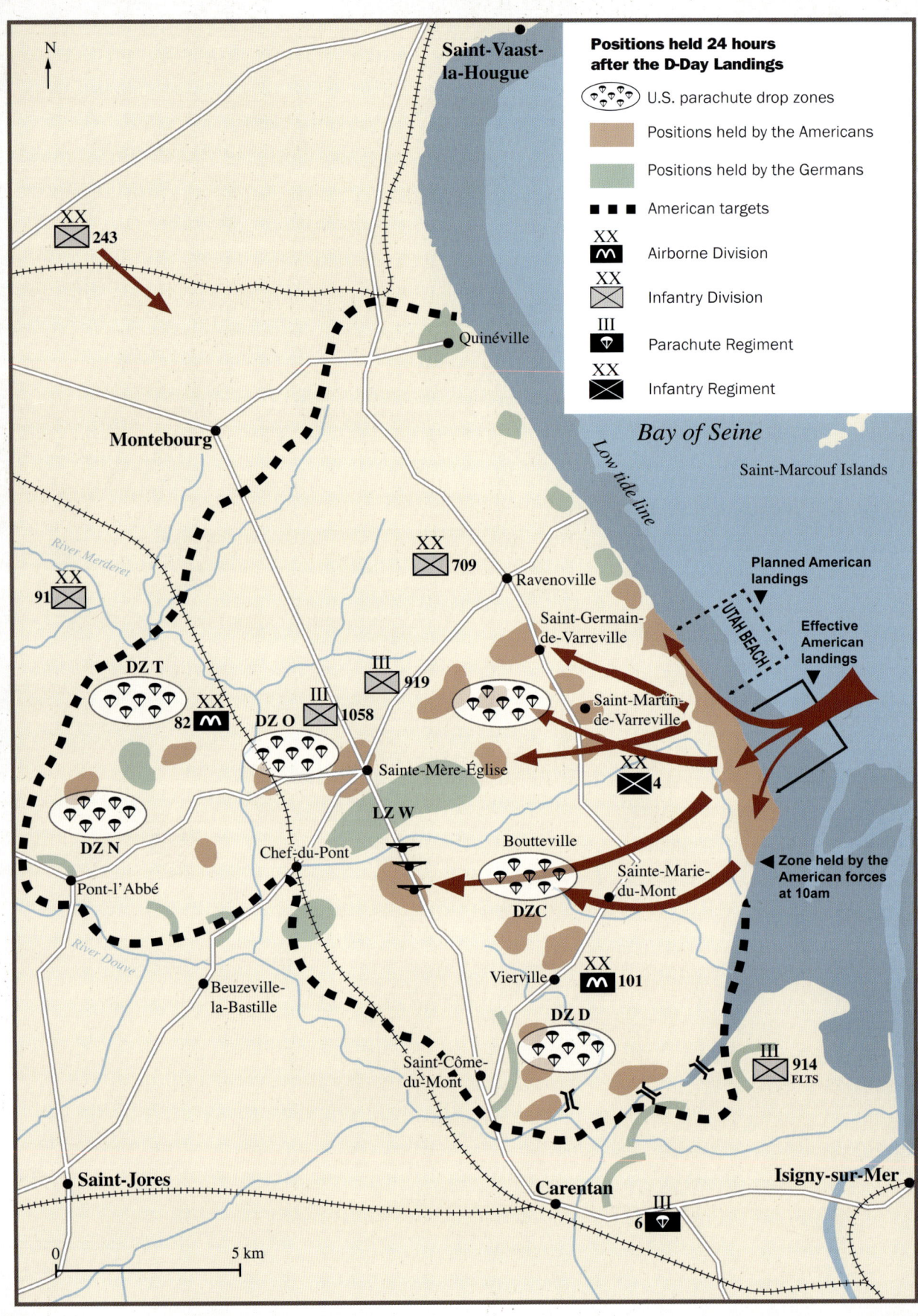

BIBLIOGRAPHY

Balkoski (Joseph), *Utah Beach, 6 juin 1944*. Histoire et Collections, 2015.

Belloc (Éric), *Objectif Sainte-Mère-Église*. Big Red One Éditions, 2016.

Department of the Army Historical Division, *Utah Beach à Cherbourg*. Foxmaster and Pozit Press, 1994.

Collectif, *Objectif Sainte-Mère*. Big Red One Éditions, 2016.

François (Dominique), *82nd Airborne Division 1917-2005*. Heimdal, 2006.

McManus (John C.), *The Americans at D-Day: The American Experience at the Normandy Invasion*. Forge Books, 2005.

Nordyke (Phil), *The All Americans in World War II*. Zenith Press, 2010.

Porcella (Thomas), *Jump Into Darkness*. 1980.

Prime (Christophe), *La Bataille du Cotentin, 6 juin-15 août 1944*. Tallandier, 2019.

Rondeau (Benoît), *Opérations aéroportées du Débarquement*. Ouest-France, 2014.

Rottman (Gordon L.), *US Airborne Units in the Mediterranean Theater 1942-44*. Osprey Publishing, 2006.

Thompson (Leroy), *The All Americans, The 82nd Airborne*. David & Charles Military Book, 1988.

Zaloga (Steven J.) et Gerrard (Howard), *Le Jour J : Utah Beach les parachutages américains*. Osprey Publishing, 2012.

ACKNOWLEDGEMENTS

The author and Editions OREP would like to thank the collectors and the museums who have contributed towards the production of this book. We would also like to thank the Airborne Museum in Sainte-Mère-Église, in particular its director, Magali Mallet.

Zone tertiaire de Nonant - 14400 BAYEUX
Tel: 02 31 51 81 31 - **Fax:** 02 31 51 81 32
E-mail: info@orepeditions.com - **Website:** www.orepeditions.com
Editor: Grégory Pique - **Editorial coordination:** Joëlle Meudic
English translation: Heather Inglis
Graphics - Layout: Antoine Salmon - **Design:** OREP Éditions
Cover credits: NARA/Life

ISBN: 978-2-8151-0552-1 - Copyright OREP 2022 - Legal Deposit: 1st quarter 2022